WHITE DEVIL

WHITE DEVIL

THE LIFE AND LEGEND OF
HUDSON TAYLOR

TIEN DAO

Translated from the Chinese edition by
K. Meikle with Jan Greenough
Compiled and illustrated by Philadelphia

MONARCH
B O O K S

Oxford, UK & Grand Rapids, Michigan, USA

Sevenoaks, UK
www.omf.org.uk

First published in 2006 in the UK by Monarch Books
(a publishing imprint of Lion Hudson plc) and OMF International,
Monarch Books, Mayfield House, 256 Banbury Road, Oxford OX2 7DH.
Tel: +44 (0) 1865 302750   Fax: +44 (0) 1865 302757
Email: monarch@lionhudson.com, www.lionhudson.com
OMF International, Station Approach, Borough Green, Sevenoaks, Kent TN15 8BG.
Tel: +44 (0) 1732 887299
email: omf@omf.org.uk, www.omf.org.uk

Distributed by:
UK: Marston Book Services Ltd, PO Box 269,
Abingdon, Oxon OX14 4YN.
USA: Kregel Publications, PO Box 2607,
Grand Rapids, Michigan 49501.

ISBN-13: 978-1-85424-773-5 (UK)
ISBN-10: 1-85424-773-5 (UK)
ISBN-13: 978-0-8254-6135-4 (USA)
ISBN-10: 0-8254-6135-9 (USA)

Author: Tien Dao
Compiler and illustrator: Po-shing Cheung, Philadelphia
Cover illustrator: Kam-shan Kwun, Philadelphia
Copyright © 2001 by Po-shing Cheung, 9th Floor,
Kwei Chow Street, Tokawawan, Kowloon, H.K. PRC
Copyright of English edition © 2006 by OMF International,
2 Cluny Road, Singapore, 259570

1st Chinese edition: February 2001
UK translation by K. Meikle with Jan Greenough

British Library Cataloguing Data
A catalogue record for this book is available from the British Library.

The text paper used in this book has been made from wood independently certified as
having come from sustainable forests.

Printed and bound in Great Britain by Cox & Wyman,Ltd, Reading.

Contents

THE SEQUENCE OF EVENTS IN THIS GRAPHIC NOVEL FOLLOWS THE
BIOGRAPHY WRITTEN BY HUDSON TAYLOR'S DESCENDANTS, AND
THE STORY IS KEPT AS LOYAL TO THAT TEXT AS POSSIBLE.

OMF International works in most East Asian countries, and among East Asian peoples around the world. It was founded by James Hudson Taylor in 1865 as the China Inland Mission. Our purpose is to glorify God through the urgent evangelisation of East Asia's billions.

In line with this, OMF Publishing seeks to motivate and equip Christians to make disciples of all peoples. Publications include:

• stories and biographies showing God at work in East Asia
• the biblical basis of mission and mission issues
• the growth and development of the church in Asia
• studies of Asian culture and religion

Books, booklets, articles and free downloads can be found on our website at *www.omf.org*

Addresses for OMF English-speaking centres can be found on page 8.

English-speaking OMF centres

Australia: PO Box 849, Epping, NSW 1710
Tel: 02 9868 4777   email: au@omf.net   www.au.omf.org

Canada: 5155 Spectrum Way, Building 21, Mississauga, ONT L4W 5A1
Toll free: 1 888 657 8010   email: omfcanada@omf.ca   www.ca.omf.org

Hong Kong: PO Box 70505, Kowloon Central PO, Hong Kong
Tel: 852 2398 1823   email: hk@omf.net   www.omf.org.hk

Malaysia: 3A Jalan Nipah, off Jalan Ampang, 55000, Kuala Lumpur
Tel: 603 4257 4263   email: my@omf.net   www.my.omf.org

New Zealand: PO Box 10159, Dominion Road, Balmoral, Auckland, 1030
Tel: 09 630 5778   email: omfnz@omf.net   www.nz.omf.org

Philippines: QCCPO Box 1997-1159, 1100 Quezon City, M.M.
Tel: 632 951 0782 email: ph-hc@omf.net   www.omf.org

Singapore: 2 Cluny Road, Singapore 259570
Tel: 65 6475 4592   email: sno@omf.net   www.sg.omf.org

UK: Station Approach, Borough Green, Sevenoaks, Kent TN15 8BG
Tel: 01732 887299   email: omf@omf.org.uk   www.omf.org.uk

USA: 10 West Dry Creek Circle, Littleton, CO 80120-4413
Toll free: 1 800 422 5330   email: omfus@omf.org   www.us.omf.org

OMF International Headquarters: 2 Cluny Road, Singapore 259570
Tel: 65 6319 4550   email: ihq@omf.net   www.omf.org

Foreword

I have been a fan of cartoons, comics and graphic novels ever since I was young – my mother often scolded me because of this! But if this format can bring to life biblical stories and spiritual characters, it will be a great tool for the younger generation. I am happy to see White Devil tell the story of Hudson Taylor in this form, and praise God for its publication.

Maak Hay Chun, General Secretary of the *Chinese Co-ordinating Centre of World Evangelism*

Forty-four years ago I read Hudson Taylor's biography and I was touched by his willingness to sacrifice his beautiful fiancée for the sake of God's calling to go to China and preach the Gospel. He proved again and again that his love for the Lord was far greater than his love of the world. I was touched by his willingness to live a life of faith, led by the Holy Spirit to give all that was left in his pocket to help the poor and needy. God in turn mightily blessed him and provided for all of his needs throughout his life. I was touched by Hudson Taylor's willingness to help rescue a drowning man. This selfless act shows us his love for the people around him, highlighting our own selfishness.

Later when I recorded some hymns for the Far East Broadcasting Company, I came across Taylor's words: "If I had a thousand lives, I would be willing to offer them to the Chinese for the sake of God. If I had a thousand pounds, I would be willing to spend it on the Chinese." He loved the Chinese people with the love of God. I am sure this book will encourage everyone, especially the younger generation, to learn from Hudson Taylor's example and turn towards the Lord. Hence I sincerely recommend this book to all.

Liu Zheng Ping, Director of *China Ministry, Baptist Union*

Preface

Many Christians have been greatly touched by Hudson Taylor's testimony. I thank the Lord for allowing me to portray Hudson's life in this format, which gives us another angle to view him from. From this we can learn of an incomparable spiritual life, totally dedicated to God. To see this complete surrender is an example for us all. I pray that this graphic novel will help us once again to realise the meaning of God's love, to come to know him more personally and so offer our lives in service to Him.

Philadelphia

"As for me and my house, we will serve the Lord." Josh 24:15

Warfare

"CONSECRATE TO ME EVERY FIRSTBORN MALE.
THE FIRST OFFSPRING OF EVERY WOMB
AMONG THE ISRAELITES BELONGS TO ME,
WHETHER MAN OR ANIMAL." EXODUS 13:2

IN RESPONSE A COUPLE WHO
LOVED THE LORD KNELT AND
DEDICATED THEIR FIRSTBORN
TO THEIR FATHER GOD

JAMES HUDSON TAYLOR WAS BORN ON 21ST MAY, 1832, IN BARNSLEY, ENGLAND.

FROM DAY ONE, HIS LIFE BELONGED TO GOD.

THE COUPLE HAD PRAYED FOR A LONG TIME FOR THIS SPECIAL BABY BOY

HUDSON WAS BOTH CLEVER AND LOVABLE. WHEN HE WAS FIVE, DISASTER HIT HIS HAPPY FAMILY. BOTH HIS YOUNGER BROTHERS DIED, LEAVING HIM AND HIS SISTER, AMELIA, TO DRAW CLOSER TO EACH OTHER.

HIS PARENTS EDUCATED HIM WELL. THEY TAUGHT HIM SELF-CONTROL, OBEDIENCE, A SENSE OF PERSONAL RESPONSIBILITY, AND CARE OVER HIS USE OF MONEY.

HUDSON

HIS DAD TAUGHT HIM TO RESPECT GOD'S WORD AND TO BELIEVE IN THE TRUTHS OF THE BIBLE.

HIS DAD PRAYED FOR HIS CHILDREN EVERY DAY AND TAUGHT THEM TO PRAY TOO.

HUDSON WENT TO SCHOOL WHEN HE WAS 11 YEARS OLD, BUT HE MISSED THE SPIRITUAL INFLUENCE OF HIS FAMILY, PARTICULARLY HIS DAD. HE ENDED UP DRIFTING AWAY FROM GOD.

AT 13 HE RETURNED BRIEFLY TO HIS CHRISTIAN LIFE, BUT AS HE GREW OLDER HE BEGAN TO DOUBT AGAIN.

ENGLISH BANK

AT THE AGE OF 15 HE WENT TO WORK IN A BANK. HE MADE NEW FRIENDS WHO LED HIM ASTRAY. HE TOSSED ASIDE HIS SPIRITUAL UPBRINGING, AND BEGAN TO SPEND MONEY FREELY ON A LIFE OF LUXURY.

HUDSON'S FAMILY SAW HIS STEADY DECLINE AND WORRIED AND PRAYED FOR HIM. AMELIA WAS UPSET, AND DECIDED TO PRAY FOR HIM THREE TIMES A DAY.

HE THOUGHT TO HIMSELF, "I'M A HOPELESS CAUSE. I MAY AS WELL ENJOY THE LIFE I'VE GOT NOW."

1849

SAVED. THANK YOU FOR LOVING ME, GOD!

CHRIST WILL BE FIRST IN FUTURE.

HUDSON OFFERED HIS LIFE MORE FULLY TO GOD. EVERYTHING CHANGED, AND HIS FRIENDSHIPS BEGAN TO IMPROVE.

NOW, HE WATCHED OUT FOR OTHERS. HE SPENT TIME IN WORSHIP AND PRAYER. HE HANDED OUT LEAFLETS TELLING OTHERS ABOUT GOD.

BUT THE DEVIL WOULDN'T LET HIM GET AWAY QUITE SO EASILY. HUDSON QUICKLY BECAME DISCOURAGED. IT TOOK TIME AND EFFORT TO READ THE BIBLE AND PRAY, AND IT WAS SO MUCH EASIER JUST TO RELAX AND HAVE FUN. HE GOT IT WRONG SO MANY TIMES, AND HUDSON WAS TOUGH ON HIMSELF, SUFFERING FOR EVERY FAILING.

BIBLE

20

HE DID THINGS HE DIDN'T MEAN TO DO. HE DIDN'T DO THE THINGS HE SHOULD.

I'M STRUGGLING SO MUCH, I FEEL SPIRITUALLY DEAD – AND THAT MAKES ME WANT TO DIE TOO.

I NEED TO FIGHT ON. FINDING GOD WILL BE THE BEST THING FOR ME, THE ONLY THING TO DO. BUT...IT'S SO CONFUSING. I WANT TO FACE GOD AND HIS HOLINESS, BUT I'M JUST NOT GOOD ENOUGH.

GOD KEPT ASKING: "WHOM CAN I SEND? WHO WILL GO FOR US?"

FINALLY, UNABLE TO OVERCOME HIS PROBLEMS BY HIMSELF, HUDSON KNEW IT WAS TIME TO WRESTLE WITH GOD AND RESOLVE THINGS.

21

FROM THAT DAY FORWARD, HUDSON LIVED A SPIRITUALLY DIRECTED LIFE. HE WAS CONSTANTLY LEARNING ABOUT CHINA, LOOKING FOR ANYTHING THAT WOULD BE HELPFUL TO HIM.

WHAT'S THIS? A BOOK, BY DR MAK. HMM...WONDER IF IT'S INTERESTING?

GOD WANTS ME TO GO TO CHINA TO TELL PEOPLE ABOUT HIM. THIS MAY BE USEFUL.

HOW ARE YOU GOING TO GET THERE?

I DON'T REALLY KNOW. I'M GOING TO FOLLOW THE EXAMPLE OF THE 12 APOSTLES AND 70 DISCIPLES. I'M NOT TAKING EXTRA MONEY OR CLOTHING. I'M GOING TO TRUST GOD TO SUPPLY EVERYTHING I NEED.

I COMPLETELY TRUST GOD AND THE INSTRUCTIONS AND PROMISES HE GAVE TO THE DISCIPLES. I DON'T BELIEVE THEY APPLIED TO THAT GENERATION ALONE. THIS IS HOW I AM GOING TO LIVE.

OTHERS DISAGREED. "HUDSON, YOUR SIMPLE TRUST IS GREAT BUT A LITTLE NAIVE! THINGS DON'T WORK THAT WAY ANY MORE."

HUDSON BEGAN STUDYING MEDICINE, BECAUSE HE KNEW THAT WOULD HELP THE CHINESE.

MY PARENTS ADVISED ME TO TAKE CARE OF MY HEALTH, BOTH SPIRITUALLY AND PHYSICALLY. IF I WAS GOING TO GO TO CHINA AS A MISSIONARY, I NEEDED TO LISTEN CAREFULLY TO GOD DURING MY PRAYER TIMES.

AS PART OF MY FITNESS REGIME I STARTED RUNNING TO GAIN STRENGTH AND STAMINA.

ARGH...IT'S HARD WORK LEARNING TO READ AND SPEAK CHINESE

WHEN I WAS 17, CHRISTMAS PROVED TO BE AN INTERESTING TIME...

AMELIA BROUGHT A FRIEND HOME. SHE WAS A MUSIC TEACHER CALLED MISS VAUGHAN, WHO LIVED IN HULL.

HUDSON THOUGHT SHE WAS VERY ATTRACTIVE. SHE THOUGHT THE SAME ABOUT HIM.

SHOULD HE STAY HERE WITH MISS VAUGHAN, OR GO TO CHINA? HE HAD TO CHOOSE.

WHEN HUDSON WAS 19 HE WENT TO HULL, TO WORK AS AN ASSISTANT TO DR HARDEY.

MISS VAUGHAN STILL COULDN'T AGREE TO HUDSON GOING TO CHINA.

LIFE WAS EVEN MORE DIFFICULT NOW THEY BOTH LIVED IN HULL. THEY GREW EVEN CLOSER.

WHY DO YOU HAVE TO GO TO CHINA? CAN'T YOU SERVE GOD JUST AS WELL LIVING IN ENGLAND?

HUDSON'S PROBLEMS SEEMED TO BE GETTING BIGGER. WHAT A CHOICE! HIS LOVE FOR MISS VAUGHAN OR SERVING GOD IN CHINA? GOD UNDERSTOOD. HE GAVE HUDSON THE CHANCE TO GO TO LONDON WITH HIS SISTER, AMELIA.

WHILE THEY WERE THERE, HUDSON MET MR PEARSE, THE SECRETARY OF THE CHINESE EVANGELISATION SOCIETY. HE INTRODUCED HIM TO ANOTHER MISSIONARY.

BACK IN HULL, DR HARDEY NEEDED HIS ROOM FOR VISITING FRIENDS, SO HUDSON MOVED OUT. HE FOUND A PLACE TO LIVE NEARBY.

SEEING SO MUCH POVERTY AROUND HIM, HUDSON DECIDED TO LIVE A LIFE THAT WOULD TEACH HIM ABOUT HARDSHIP AND DISCIPLINE.

HUDSON ATE ONLY WHEAT AND RICE EACH DAY. HE SPENT MOST OF HIS MONEY IN HELPING THE POOR. AT LAST HE FELT HE WAS DOING THE RIGHT THING.

SATAN WAS NOT HAPPY ABOUT HUDSON'S PROGRESS WITH GOD.

MISS VAUGHAN GAVE HIM A FINAL WARNING THAT THEIR RELATIONSHIP WAS FALLING APART.

HUDSON, I'M NOT COMING TO CHINA WITH YOU.

IF YOU WANT TO CONTINUE OUR ENGAGEMENT, YOU MUST PROMISE THAT YOU'LL STAY HERE. IF YOU MUST GO TO CHINA, PLEASE LEAVE ME ALONE!

SATAN'S WORK WAS VERY REAL. HUDSON'S HEART ACHED. "SURELY IT ISN'T WORTH SACRIFICING THE PERSON YOU LOVE THE MOST? WHY DO I HAVE TO BE THE ONE WHO GOES TO CHINA?"

GOD'S PROMISES SEEMED SO ABSTRACT - AND MISS VAUGHAN WAS SO REAL. "FORGET CHINA! SURELY IT WOULD BE JUST AS GOOD TO STAY AND SERVE GOD HERE WITH HER BY HIS SIDE?"

BUT HE REMEMBERED GOD'S EVERLASTING LOVE AND FORGIVENESS. HOW COULD HE TURN AWAY FROM THAT LOVE FOR SOMEONE ELSE?

MY HEART MAGNIFIES THE LORD. MY SOUL DELIGHTS IN GOD MY SAVIOUR

I CONSIDER EVERYTHING A LOSS COMPARED TO THE SURPASSING GREATNESS OF KNOWING CHRIST JESUS MY LORD, FOR WHOSE SAKE I HAVE LOST ALL THINGS. I CONSIDER THEM RUBBISH THAT I MAY GAIN CHRIST.

AFTER MUCH THOUGHT AND PRAYER HUDSON SACRIFICED HIS FEELINGS FOR THE SAKE OF HIS CALLING.

ONCE, DR HARDEY FORGOT TO GIVE HIM HIS WAGES. HUDSON DECIDED NOT TO REMIND HIM

GOD WAS WITH HIM.

MON
TUE
WED
THU
FAI
SAT

HUDSON KNEW THAT IN CHINA HE WOULD BE QUITE ALONE. HE KNEW THAT HE HAD TO STRENGTHEN HIS FAITH IF HE WANTED TO FULFIL HIS LIFE'S GOAL.

HE HAD ALREADY DECIDED NOT TO ASK PEOPLE FOR HELP. HE WANTED GOD TO MEET HIS EVERY NEED, AND MOVE OTHER PEOPLE TO DO WHAT WAS NEEDED.

"THERE WAS REAL WARFARE IN MY SPIRIT. I FELT REALLY LOW.

ONCE I HAD PRAYED, I SAW WHAT A HYPOCRITE I WAS. I HAD BOASTED THAT I WAS WILLING TO TRUST GOD, BUT I WASN'T WILLING TO GIVE HIM ONE COIN."

ONE THOUGHT KEPT COMING BACK: "ASK, AND IT WILL BE GIVEN."

THEN THE POOR MAN SAID TO ME, "SIR, HAVE PITY ON US, FOR HIS SAKE."

THANK GOD. HIS HOLY SPIRIT REALLY HELPED ME THROUGH THAT STRUGGLE. NOW MY HEART IS AT PEACE AND I CAN TRULY PRAISE GOD.

THIS SMALL AMOUNT OF MONEY WON'T GO FAR BUT IT'S ALL I HAVE. NOW I CAN SAY THE WORDS AND BELIEVE THEM TOO. I KNOW I CAN TRUST MY FATHER GOD.

TO MY SURPRISE AND PLEASURE, THE FOLLOWING MORNING I FOUND A BOWL OF STEAMING HOT PORRIDGE OUTSIDE MY FRONT DOOR!

KNOCK, KNOCK

NEXT THE LANDLORD HANDED ME A LETTER.

INSIDE WAS A COIN WORTH FOUR OF MY HALF-CROWNS!

WOW! A THREE HUNDRED PER CENT RETURN! THANK YOU, GOD!

GOD'S PERFECT TIMING GAVE ME A TREMENDOUS LIFT, BUT DR HARDEY STILL HADN'T REMEMBERED TO PAY ME.

I KNOW THAT IF I REMIND HIM, IT MEANS I'M NOT TRUSTING GOD.

I STILL FEEL THAT GOD WANTS ME TO WAIT, TO SAY NOTHING.

HUDSON, ISN'T IT TIME FOR YOUR WAGES?

HARRUMPH. YOU DIDN'T REMIND ME ABOUT YOUR PAY, AND NOW I'VE BANKED ALL THE CASH. I WOULD HAVE PAID YOU IF I'D REMEMBERED.

AFTER SOME TIME...

OH NO, THE MEDICINE IS BOILING OVER!

BUBBLE, BUBBLE.

HUDSON ARRIVED IN LONDON TO TRAIN AS A DOCTOR.

HE CONTINUED TO RELY ON GOD'S GRACE AND PROMISES, AND FOUND THAT ALL HIS NEEDS WERE MET. ONCE HE CAUGHT A SERIOUS INFECTION, AND BECAME SO ILL THAT EVERYONE THOUGHT HE WOULD DIE. HIS OWN DOCTOR EVEN ARRANGED A FUNERAL SERVICE FOR HIM. BUT HUDSON HAD FAITH. HE BELIEVED THAT HE WOULD NOT DIE BEFORE HE HAD COMPLETED HIS LIFE'S WORK. EVENTUALLY HE RECOVERED, TELLING THE PESSIMISTIC DOCTOR THAT GOD HAD BEEN IN CONTROL ALL THE TIME. HE PRAISED GOD FOR HIS RETURN TO HEALTH.

HUDSON WENT THROUGH MANY TRIALS, AND THROUGH THEM HE LEARNED TO TRUST GOD COMPLETELY.

A MAN CALLED HUNG SIU-TSUEN WAS WORKING IN CHINESE CHURCHES IN BRITAIN. AS A RESULT OF HIS WORK, MANY MISSIONARIES WERE BEING SENT OUT TO CHINA.

HUDSON WENT TO SEE MR BIRD, THE SECRETARY OF THE CHINA EVANGELISATION SOCIETY.

IF YOU HAVE DECIDED TO GO TO CHINA, THERE IS LITTLE REASON FOR YOU TO KEEP PRACTISING MEDICINE. CHOOSE ANOTHER SKILL WHICH WILL BE OF USE.

IT COSTS ABOUT £60 FOR A SINGLE MAN TO GO TO CHINA. THIS WOULD BE A GOOD TIME FOR YOU TO GAIN A CERTIFICATE IN OPHTHALMOLOGY.

I AM VERY HAPPY TO RECOMMEND YOU TO THE BOARD.

DEAR MOTHER, WITH MR BIRD'S HELP I HAVE RESOLVED ALL THE OUTSTANDING ISSUES. I AM NOW AWAITING THEIR REPLY, AND THEN I'LL BE ABLE TO GO TO CHINA. PLEASE PRAY FOR ME.

I AM WILLING TO GIVE UP EVERYTHING FOR CHRIST.

HUDSON SAILED TO CHINA FROM LIVERPOOL.

I WILL NEITHER SPARE MY LIFE NOR TREAT IT AS PRECIOUS. I WILL ONLY ASPIRE TO FINISH MY JOURNEY, TO FULFIL THE MINISTRY I RECEIVED FROM THE LORD JESUS TO TESTIFY TO GOD'S GRACE AND MERCY.

MY PARENTS AND PASTOR CAME TO PRAY FOR ME AND SEE ME OFF.

DEAR MOTHER, DON'T CRY... I'M GOING FOR A GREAT REASON, TO TAKE THE GOSPEL OF THE LORD TO THE POOR CHINESE PEOPLE. THEY ARE DESPERATE FOR THE KNOWLEDGE OF HIS LOVE.

MOTHER'S TEARS WENT THROUGH ME LIKE A KNIFE. ONLY THEN DID I FULLY UNDERSTAND THE VERSE: "FOR GOD SO LOVED THE WORLD THAT HE GAVE HIS ONLY BEGOTTEN SON."

SATURDAY 24TH SEPTEMBER 1853

DARK CLOUDS WERE GATHERING AND THE WIND WAS PICKING UP. A VIOLENT STORM WAS COMING. IT WAS AN AWFUL SIGHT ...

"THE SHIP CANNOT WITHSTAND THIS BATTERING. BY TOMORROW THERE WILL ONLY BE A FEW PLANKS LEFT FLOATING."

EVERYONE IS HOPING WE WILL SURVIVE THE STORM. ONLY GOD CAN RESCUE US.

IF YOU SEEK ME IN TROUBLE I WILL RESCUE YOU AND YOU WILL GLORIFY ME.

LORD, IF IT IS POSSIBLE TAKE THIS CUP FROM ME.

THE SHIP PASSED BY THE EAST INDIAN ISLANDS AND ON INTO THE PACIFIC OCEAN TOWARDS CHINA. I JOINED THE SAILORS WORSHIPPING GOD DURING THE JOURNEY.

JANUARY 1854

THANK GOD, THE SHIP ESCAPED THE STORM. WE PASSED THE CAPE OF GOOD HOPE, KEEPING AWAY FROM THE DEADLY ROCKS.

MARCH 1854

HUDSON LANDED IN SHANGHAI. THERE WAS NO ONE THERE TO MEET HIM OR NOTICE HIS ARRIVAL.

MY HEART WAS FULL OF GLADNESS AND THANKS. THE LORD HAD RESCUED ME FROM MANY DANGERS SO THAT I COULD SET FOOT IN CHINA. NOW I WAS FACING STRANGE FACES AND STRANGE PLACES WITH MY FAMILY MILES BEHIND...

BECAUSE YOU ARE MY ROCK AND FORTRESS, I BEG YOU TO GUIDE ME AND TO INSTRUCT ME FOR YOUR NAME'S SAKE.

I HAD THREE LETTERS OF INTRODUCTION TO CONTACTS IN CHINA. BUT WHEN I WENT TO THE FIRST TWO ADDRESSES, I FOUND THAT THE PEOPLE THEY WERE MEANT FOR HAD BOTH DIED. THERE WAS ONLY ONE NAME LEFT ... I NEEDED TO TRUST IN THE LORD'S GUIDANCE AGAIN.

41

AT THAT TIME THE CHAOS IN SHANGHAI WAS ALMOST OVERWHELMING. THERE WAS GREAT POVERTY AND SUFFERING. THE CONSTANT SOUND OF BOMBING EXHAUSTED HUDSON. HE COULDN'T UNDERSTAND THE LANGUAGE, LET ALONE CONVEY THE GOSPEL TO ANYONE, WHICH LEFT HIM DEEPLY DISCOURAGED. OTHER EUROPEANS IN SHANGHAI LIVED COMFORTABLY AND LOOKED DOWN ON HIM, CAUSING HIM FURTHER MISERY.

IN DAYTIME THE SUMMER HEAT FELT LIKE A SAUNA. THE NIGHT BROUGHT FURTHER MISERY FROM THE CONSTANT ATTACKS BY MOSQUITOES, SUCKING HIS BLOOD LIKE LEECHES.

THEN THE CHINESE EVANGELISATION SOCIETY SENT OUT A MISSIONARY FAMILY – THE PARKERS – AND HUDSON PROMISED TO CARE FOR THEM.

HE WAS ALREADY LIVING OFF THE GENEROSITY OF OTHERS. HOW WAS HE MEANT TO PROVIDE FOR ANOTHER FAMILY?

42

THE LORD HELPED HUDSON TO FIND A HOUSE IN THE NORTH GATE. ALTHOUGH IT WAS VERY RUN DOWN IT WAS AT LEAST HIS OWN. HE WAS VERY THANKFUL.

HUDSON MOVED INTO HIS NEW HOUSE IN AUGUST, AND STARTED WORK IN SEPTEMBER. HE SET UP A DAILY MOBILE SCHOOL WITH MR CHUI, A CHRISTIAN TEACHER. BIBLE STUDY AND PRAYER WERE INCLUDED IN THE CURRICULUM.

DAILY MOBILE SCHOOL

走讀日學

HUDSON WAS RESPONSIBLE FOR RUNNING A CLINIC AND MANY PATIENTS CAME EVERY DAY. TEN PEOPLE CAME TO THE FAMILY WORSHIP.

診所

CLINIC

禮拜

WORSHIP

HUDSON AND MR CHUI WENT OUT TOGETHER TO HAND OUT GOSPEL TRACTS.

43

THE DAY OF DR PARKER'S ARRIVAL IN SHANGHAI WAS GETTING CLOSER. I STILL HADN'T FOUND A PLACE FOR THEM TO STAY.

HUDSON WAS STILL SEARCHING FOR ROOMS FOR A FAMILY, WHEN HE HEARD THAT MRS BURTON HAD DIED. MR BURTON WANTED TO RENT OUT HIS HOUSE. WITH GOD'S HELP, HUDSON WAS ABLE TO TAKE THE HOUSE.

AT LEAST IT'S SOMEWHERE FOR THE PARKERS TO STAY!

WELCOME TO CHINA.

DECEMBER 1854

JIANGSU

CHONG MING

WUSHONG

GSHAN   SHUNGJING   WANGPU RIVER

JIAXING

HUDSON AND EDKINS SET OUT FROM SHANGHAI TO MAKE A SERIES OF JOURNEYS BY BOAT AROUND THE COAST. THEY PREACHED THE GOSPEL TO THE MONKS LIVING THERE.

THE PEOPLE WELCOMED WESTERN DOCTORS AND THEIR EFFECTIVE MODERN WESTERN MEDICINE.

THE GOSPEL ATTRACTED MANY PEOPLE WHO CAME TO LEARN MORE ABOUT GOD. THEY WANTED TO DISCUSS THE BIBLE, TRYING TO UNDERSTAND THE TRUTH.

CROWDS GATHERED BECAUSE MANY PEOPLE HAD NEVER SEEN FOREIGNERS BEFORE. THERE WERE LOTS OF OPPORTUNITIES TO MAKE FRIENDS AND TALK.

EARLY 1855

WUSHONG

JIADING

CHINGPU

WANGPU RIVER

CHUANSAH

SONGJIANG

NAHUI

CHINGSHEN

HUDSON ENJOYED HIS TRAVELS BY BOAT. HE KNEW HE WAS DOING GOD'S WILL.

WE PREACH, TEACH, TREAT THE SICK AND GIVE THEM MEDICINE. THERE ARE ALWAYS LOTS OF PEOPLE IN NEED.

ON HIS FIFTH JOURNEY OUT TO CHONG MING, HUDSON TRAVELLED WITH A FRIEND CALLED POULTON.

AT HAI MEN THEY RENTED A CART. IT MADE CARRYING THEIR BOOKS MUCH EASIER.

NANG TONG
△ LANG SHAN
HAI MEN
LU SHAN △ CHONG MING
YANGTZE RIVER

WE MUST BRING THE GOSPEL TO CHINA. PEOPLE NEED TO KNOW THE GRACE OF GOD.

ONE DAY THEY TOOK A BOAT TO LANG SHAN AND CLIMBED THE MOUNTAIN. THEY WERE STUNNED BY THE WONDERFUL VIEW OF RIVERS, TEMPLES AND VILLAGES. IT MADE HUDSON THINK OF MOSES LOOKING AT CANAAN FROM MOUNT SINAI.

THERE WERE SOLDIERS CAUSING TROUBLE AROUND THE SOUTH OF TONG ZHOU. OUR SERVANTS WERE NERVOUS, AND LEFT US. BUT WE CARRIED ON BY THE GRACE OF GOD, TAKING EVERY OPPORTUNITY TO PREACH THE GOSPEL.

ONE DAY WE WERE SURROUNDED BY A CROWD.

WE WERE BEATEN AND THROWN TO THE GROUND SEVERAL TIMES, AND THEN DRAGGED OFF TO THE TONG ZHOU COUNTY OFFICE.

WE WERE DRAGGED AND JOSTLED THE WHOLE WAY. WHEN WE ARRIVED AT THE OFFICE WE HANDED OVER OUR NAME CARDS.

BEFORE LONG, WE WERE TAKEN INSIDE TO MEET THE COUNTY MAGISTRATE, MR CHENG.

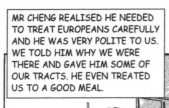

MR CHENG REALISED HE NEEDED TO TREAT EUROPEANS CAREFULLY AND HE WAS VERY POLITE TO US. WE TOLD HIM WHY WE WERE THERE AND GAVE HIM SOME OF OUR TRACTS. HE EVEN TREATED US TO A GOOD MEAL.

HE ALSO ALLOWED US TO GO INTO TOWN AND TO PREACH. LATER, WHEN WE RETURNED TO OUR LITTLE BOAT, WE THANKED GOD.

MAY 1855

OVER SIX OUTREACHES, WE GAVE AWAY NEARLY 13,000 BOOKS AND TRACTS TO THE CHINESE AROUND US.

FU SHANG

LIU HE

JIA DIN

CHAN SHU

HEN JIN

ON THE SIXTH JOURNEY HUDSON TRAVELLED ALONG THE YANGTZE RIVER, TREATING THE SICK AND PREACHING ALONG THE WAY.

Frontiers

Hudson aged 21–23

HUDSON, PARKER AND POULTON DECIDED TO GO TO NINGBO (IN ZHEJIANG PROVINCE) TO PREACH. ON THEIR WAY, THEY MET THE DYER SISTERS ON BOARD A BOAT. THE SISTERS WERE BOTH BELIEVERS.

JUNE 1856

MEANWHILE, PARKER HAD BEEN ASSIGNED TO ESTABLISH A HOSPITAL IN NINGBO. HUDSON WAS LEFT ALONE.

IN AUGUST HUDSON RECEIVED A LETTER TELLING HIM TO MOVE OUT OF HIS HOME, BECAUSE TWO NEW MISSIONARIES WOULD NEED IT.

BUT GOD HAD ALREADY STARTED MAKING NEW PLANS FOR HUDSON. HE MET A MAN WHO WAS SELLING A HOUSE; THEY STRUCK A DEAL AND HUDSON WAS ABLE TO BUY IT.

IN ORDER TO BUILD RELATIONSHIPS WITH THE CHINESE PEOPLE MORE EASILY, HUDSON DECIDED HE NEEDED TO LOOK MORE LIKE THEM. HE DYED HIS HAIR BLACK AND STARTED GROWING A LONG PONYTAIL. BEFORE HIS HAIR WAS LONG ENOUGH HE ATTACHED A FAKE ONE.

ON THE EVENING OF 23RD AUGUST HE TRANSFORMED HIMSELF FOR THE FIRST TIME INTO A "CHINESE MAN".

"SINCE I STARTED WEARING THE SAME AS MY CHINESE FRIENDS, PEOPLE SEEM TO BE A LOT MORE AT EASE WITH ME."

"HOWEVER, OTHER WESTERNERS LAUGH AT ME AND CRITICISE ME FOR GIVING UP MY WESTERN CLOTHING. THEY DON'T WANT TO HAVE ANYTHING TO DO WITH ME. ONLY THE LORD CAN GIVE ME PEACE AND JOY. I WAS OVERJOYED WHEN MY SERVANT GAVE HIS LIFE TO THE LORD AND WAS BAPTISED. PARKER OFTEN WRITES TO ME FROM NINGBO AND HIS LETTERS ARE ENCOURAGING. THEY MAKE ME FEEL THAT GOD WOULD NEVER LEAVE ME ALONE."

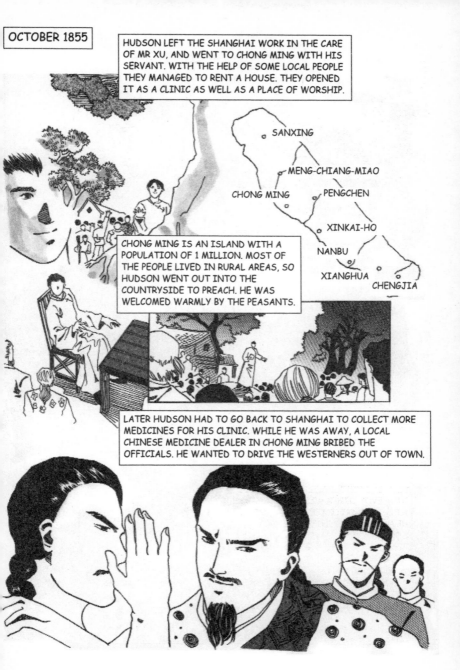

OCTOBER 1855

HUDSON LEFT THE SHANGHAI WORK IN THE CARE OF MR XU, AND WENT TO CHONG MING WITH HIS SERVANT. WITH THE HELP OF SOME LOCAL PEOPLE THEY MANAGED TO RENT A HOUSE. THEY OPENED IT AS A CLINIC AS WELL AS A PLACE OF WORSHIP.

SANXING

MENG-CHIANG-MIAO

CHONG MING

PENGCHEN

XINKAI-HO

NANBU

XIANGHUA

CHENGJIA

CHONG MING IS AN ISLAND WITH A POPULATION OF 1 MILLION. MOST OF THE PEOPLE LIVED IN RURAL AREAS, SO HUDSON WENT OUT INTO THE COUNTRYSIDE TO PREACH. HE WAS WELCOMED WARMLY BY THE PEASANTS.

LATER HUDSON HAD TO GO BACK TO SHANGHAI TO COLLECT MORE MEDICINES FOR HIS CLINIC. WHILE HE WAS AWAY, A LOCAL CHINESE MEDICINE DEALER IN CHONG MING BRIBED THE OFFICIALS. HE WANTED TO DRIVE THE WESTERNERS OUT OF TOWN.

IT WASN'T EASY FOR THE OFFICIALS IN CHONG MING TO DRIVE HIM OUT, BUT THEY FOUND A WAY. WHEN HUDSON WAS IN SHANGHAI IN DECEMBER, HE RECEIVED A LETTER FROM THE BRITISH CONSULATE. IT SAID THAT HUDSON'S ACTIVITIES VIOLATED AN AGREEMENT BETWEEN THE CHINESE AND BRITISH GOVERNMENTS. HE WENT TO THE CONSULATE OFFICE.

"HUDSON, MOVE OUT OF CHONG MING STRAIGHT AWAY."

I WAS DEEPLY WORRIED. I DIDN'T WANT TO LEAVE MY PEOPLE, BUT I DIDN'T WANT TO CAUSE TROUBLE EITHER.

"DUE TO THE RESTRICTIONS OF THE CHINESE-BRITISH AGREEMENT, HUDSON TAYLOR MUST MOVE OUT OF CHONG MING IMMEDIATELY, OR BEAR THE CONSEQUENCES."

"FATHER, MAY YOUR NAME BE GLORIFIED."

THE FATHER IN HEAVEN HAS GIVEN ALL POWER TO JESUS CHRIST.

IT SHOULD BE AN EASY THING IF THE LORD WANTS YOU TO PREACH IN CHONG MING.

HUDSON WAS FORCED OUT OF CHONG MING BY THE ORDER OF THE CONSULATE, BUT HE WAS NOT CONVINCED. HE TRIED TO APPEAL, BUT THE CONSULATE WAS NOT IN SHANGHAI AT THE TIME.

WHY DO I HAVE TO DEPEND ON THE GOVERNMENT? THE LORD SHOULD GUIDE ME.

I WILL NOT BE DEPENDENT ON OTHERS, BUT RELY ON GOD AND FOLLOW HIS DIRECTION.

A NEW MISSIONARY, CALLED BEN WILLIAM, ARRIVED.

"ARE YOU HUDSON TAYLOR?"

Jehovah Jireh

Hudson aged 24–28

BEN WILLIAM WAS AN EXPERIENCED MISSIONARY. HE WAS CHOSEN BY GOD, AND BECAME A GOOD FRIEND TO HUDSON.

THEY SUPPORTED EACH OTHER AS THEY PREACHED IN NANG XUN IN ZHEJIANG PROVINCE.

SCHOOLS

TEMPLES

TEAHOUSES

THEY ALL BECAME POPULAR PLACES FOR PREACHING THE GOSPEL. SOON WILLIAM TOOK TO WEARING CHINESE CLOTHES TOO, AND THE PEOPLE LOVED HIM FOR THIS.

"WE WATCHED FAMILIES GATHER TO LISTEN TO OUR STORIES ABOUT JESUS WHO DIED FOR US ALL. WE COULD HARDLY HOLD BACK OUR TEARS OF GRATITUDE TO GOD."

WILLIAM'S STRONG FAITH SEEMED TO BE A SPECIAL GIFT FROM GOD. HIS FRIENDSHIP HELPED HUDSON TO FEEL THAT HE UNDERSTOOD HIMSELF BETTER.

WORKING TOGETHER WITH WILLIAM, HUDSON FELT A NEW STRENGTH. HE KNEW THAT GOD HAD SENT A FRIEND TO ENCOURAGE HIM, AND TOGETHER THEY MADE GREAT STRIDES FORWARD.

ONE DAY IN WU DIAN, ZHEJIANG PROVINCE, A GANG THREATENED THEM. THEY DEMANDED 10 SILVER DOLLARS OR A PIECE OF OPIUM. OTHERWISE THEY WOULD VANDALISE THE MISSIONARIES' BOAT.

WISE MEN THINK ALIKE. HUDSON AND WILLIAM KEPT PRAYING, ATTACKING SATAN'S TERRITORY IN JESUS' NAME. THE VICTORY WOULD ULTIMATELY BE HIS.

WHEN THE BOATMAN HEARD OF THE THREATS, HE QUICKLY TOOK THE BOAT OUT OF THE PORT AND HID WITH HUDSON AND WILLIAM.

THE FIFTY GANGSTERS WERE LOOKING AROUND BUT FOUND NOTHING.

"WHERE IS THE BOAT?"

"WHERE ARE THE FOREIGNERS?"

SAVED BY THE BOATMAN, THEY SPENT THE NIGHT ON THE BOAT, PRAYING AND THANKING GOD.

FEBRUARY 1856. HUDSON GOT TO KNOW A BOAT OWNER CALLED BAO WA SHI, A BELIEVER FROM SHANG TOU. AS THEY TALKED, HUDSON FELT GOD CALLING HIM TO GO BACK TO SHANG TOU.

THE FOLLOWING DAY, HUDSON'S KNEES AND FEET HURT REALLY BADLY. THE GANG WAS STILL LOOKING FOR THEM. THEY DECIDED TO LEAVE WU DIAN AND GO BACK TO SHANGHAI.

60

"I COULD NOT SHAKE OFF THIS FEELING THAT GOD WAS CALLING ME TO SHANG TOU. FINALLY I ASKED WILLIAM TO COME INTO MY ROOM AND TOLD HIM ABOUT MY CONVICTION."

"I WAS WORRIED THAT IT MEANT WE MUST PART, BUT TO MY SURPRISE, WILLIAM FELT THE SAME CALLING. WE KNEW IT WAS GOD'S WILL. WE DECIDED TO GO TO SHANG TOU TO MEET BAO WA SHI AS SOON AS POSSIBLE."

WE ARRANGED TO STAY ABOVE A CANDLE AND INCENSE STORE.

IN MARCH, WE ARRIVED IN SHANG TOU.

AT THE TIME, SHANG TOU WAS A MAJOR PORT FOR OPIUM SMUGGLING. IT WAS A HUGE PROBLEM. SMUGGLERS TOOK OPIUM BY BOAT TO CUBA AND KOLOW – AND USUALLY A THIRD OF THE CREW WOULD DIE DURING THE JOURNEY.

LOCAL PEOPLE HATED WESTERNERS, BECAUSE THEY WERE USUALLY BEHIND THE TERRIBLE OPIUM TRADE. OUR TIME THERE WAS DIFFICULT.

WE COULD ONLY DEPEND ON THE LORD AND KEEP PRAYING. WE HOPED OUR PRAYERS AND GOD'S LOVE WOULD CHANGE THE WAY PEOPLE RESPONDED TO US.

MEANWHILE, HUDSON CURED A GOVERNMENT OFFICIAL WHO WAS SICK. IN GRATITUDE, THE MAN HELPED HIM TO SET UP A CLINIC. HUDSON RETURNED TO SHANGHAI TO COLLECT THE MEDICINES HE NEEDED.

GOD'S GARDEN IS VERY BIG, BUT HE DOESN'T PUT ALL THE GARDENERS IN ONE PLACE. WILLIAM AND HUDSON PARTED, BUT SOON AFTERWARDS, WILLIAM WAS ARRESTED.

WE BELIEVE THAT ALL THINGS ARE PLANNED BY THE LORD. THOSE WHO TRUST HIM MAY REJOICE.

"WHILST PASSING SHI MEN, WE GOT LOST. THE PORTERS WHO WERE HELPING WITH THE LUGGAGE GAVE UP AND LEFT US. MY SERVANT WENT AHEAD TO CHANG AN TO LOOK FOR MORE HELPERS."

HUDSON FELT SURROUNDED BY TROUBLES. HE ARRIVED IN SHANGHAI ONLY TO FIND THAT THE CLINIC HAD BEEN BURNED TO THE GROUND. HE TRAVELLED ON TO MEET UP WITH PARKER, WHO HE KNEW WOULD HELP HIM.

"WHEN I ARRIVED IN CHANG AN I WAITED UNTIL EVENING FOR MY SERVANT, BUT HE DIDN'T COME."

IT WAS GETTING DARKER. I ASKED PEOPLE ABOUT MY SERVANT, AND THEY TOLD ME HE HAD LEFT, HEADING TOWARDS HAI NING.

"I WAS WORRIED, AND MY LEGS WERE HURTING ME. I DECIDED TO STAY OVERNIGHT IN CHANG AN AND CARRY ON TRAVELLING THE NEXT DAY.

HAI NING

"WHEN I ARRIVED IN HAI NING THE NEXT DAY, I STILL COULDN'T FIND MY SERVANT. I COULDN'T EVEN FIND A PLACE TO STAY THAT NIGHT. I EVENTUALLY RESTED ON SOME TEMPLE STEPS."

"I WAS JUST ABOUT TO FALL ASLEEP WHEN A TRAMP CAME AND TRIED TO STEAL MY MONEY. I STARTED PRAYING FOR THE LORD'S PROTECTION."

I HEARD FOOTSTEPS ...

THEN I HEARD ANOTHER MAN APPROACHING.

"WHAT DO YOU WANT?"

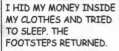

I HID MY MONEY INSIDE MY CLOTHES AND TRIED TO SLEEP. THE FOOTSTEPS RETURNED.

"I'M ONLY HERE TO PROTECT YOU."

"I DON'T NEED YOUR PROTECTION. I WORSHIP THE TRUE GOD AND HE PROTECTS ME. I KNOW WHAT YOU WANT AND I WON'T LET YOU GET IT."

THE TWO TRAMPS LEFT AND CAME BACK AGAIN WITH A THIRD. THEY CAME TO CHECK IF I WAS ASLEEP.

"DON'T EVEN THINK ABOUT IT! I'M AWAKE!"

I DIDN'T DARE GO TO SLEEP SO I STARTED SINGING SONGS AND PRAYING ALOUD. THIS KEPT THEM AWAY. THEY FINALLY LEFT AT DAWN.

THANK GOD.

I THANKED GOD AND GOT SOME SLEEP.

SHI MEN
HAI NIN
HAI YAN
CHANG AN
YU HAN
HANGZHOU

THE GRAND CANAL RUNS FROM BEIJING TO HANGZHOU.

I DECIDED TO GO BACK TO CHANG AN. ON THE WAY, I THOUGHT ABOUT GOD'S LOVE AND GRACE, ASKING HIS FORGIVENESS FOR MY MISTAKES.

AT FIRST I COULDN'T FIND A BOAT AT THE PORT OF SHI MEN. LUCKILY A BOATMAN HELPED ME FIND ONE, AND I SET OFF TO SHANGHAI.

IN SHANGHAI I DISCOVERED THAT MY SERVANT HAD STOLEN MY LUGGAGE. I WONDERED WHAT JESUS WOULD HAVE DONE IN THIS SITUATION. IN THE END I WROTE HIM A LETTER SAYING THAT I FORGAVE HIM, AND ASKED HIM IF HE WOULD CONSIDER RETURNING MY FOREIGN BOOKS TO ME.

IN AUGUST, HUDSON WENT BACK TO NINGBO, WHERE HE MET UP WITH HIS
FRIENDS JOHNSON AND DARWIN. PARKER PREPARED ENOUGH MEDICINE FOR THEM
TO TAKE TO THEIR CLINIC. HUDSON WAS EAGER TO GET BACK TO SHANG TOU.

WHEN PASSING THROUGH SHANGHAI, JOHNSON AND DARWIN
ASKED HUDSON TO WAIT FOR A WHILE TO SEE IF THEY COULD
JOIN HIM. HE WAITED UNTIL OCTOBER. THEY FINALLY MET
WITH BAO WA SHI AND HEADED FOR SHANG TOU.

"A LETTER
FOR YOU, MR
TAYLOR."

"WHAT?
WILLIAM
ARRESTED!"

HUDSON WAS DISMAYED WHEN HE HEARD OF
WILLIAM'S ARREST. HE SEEMED TO BE
SURROUNDED WITH TROUBLE: MEDICINES
DESTROYED, LUGGAGE STOLEN, LIVES IN
DANGER, AND DIFFICULTIES WITH TRAVEL.
WAS THE DOOR TO SHANG TOU CLOSING?

AFTER ALL HIS PREPARATIONS, HUDSON COULDN'T GO TO SHANG TOU. INSTEAD PARKER ARRANGED FOR HIM TO SETTLE IN WU JIA QIAO, A VILLAGE NEXT TO NINGBO. THIS EVENTUALLY BECAME THE FIRST HOME BASE OF THE CHINA INLAND MISSION.

JOHNSON'S FRIENDS THE DYER SISTERS WERE TEACHING AT A SCHOOL NEARBY. THESE WERE THE GIRLS HUDSON HAD MET ON THE BOAT. HE REALISED THAT HE WAS FALLING IN LOVE WITH MARIA, THE YOUNGER SISTER.

CHEN HAI
NAN AOU
CHAO YAN • SHANG TOU
HAI MEN •
HUI DON •

LATER THEY UNDERSTOOD WHY GOD HADN'T LET THEM GO TO SHANG TOU. A BRITISH GUNSHIP HAD ATTACKED THE GUANGZHOU DISTRICT, CAUSING AN OUTBREAK OF VIOLENCE AGAINST ALL BRITISH PEOPLE LIVING IN THE AREA.

THE CANTONESE PEOPLE LIVING IN NINGBO BECAME VERY ANTI-WESTERN. IN ORDER TO PREVENT MORE TROUBLE, MOST OF THE WESTERN WOMEN DECIDED TO MOVE TO SHANGHAI FOR A WHILE. HUDSON WAS ASSIGNED TO ACCOMPANY THEM, BUT THE DYER SISTERS DECIDED TO STAY AT THE SCHOOL IN NINGBO. HUDSON FOUND IT HARD TO BE APART FROM MARIA.

HE THOUGHT THAT BEING SO FAR APART MIGHT CHANGE HIS FEELINGS FOR MARIA, BUT HE FOUND HE MISSED HER DESPERATELY. JOHNSON SAW HIS HEARTACHE AND SUGGESTED THAT HE SHOULD WRITE TO MARIA AND PROPOSE.

MARIA WAS OVERJOYED WHEN SHE RECEIVED THE LETTER. SHE WENT TO HER HEAD TEACHER TO ASK FOR HER APPROVAL. HOWEVER, THE HEAD TEACHER DISAPPROVED. SHE ORDERED HER TO WRITE A REFUSAL. MARIA WAS SAD, BUT FELT SHE MUST LEAVE THE MATTER IN THE LORD'S HANDS.

HUDSON WAS HEARTBROKEN WHEN HE RECEIVED MARIA'S REPLY. JOHNSON TRIED TO COMFORT HIM.

THE SITUATION IN NINGBO STARTED TO CALM DOWN, AND HUDSON DECIDED TO RETURN THERE. HOWEVER, HE HAD ALREADY DECIDED TO RESIGN FROM THE LONDON MISSIONARY SOCIETY. HE DISAGREED WITH THE WAY THE SOCIETY BORROWED MONEY TO PAY WAGES, AND FELT THIS WAS AGAINST GOD'S TEACHING.

THE SOCIETY ACCEPTED HIS RESIGNATION. HUDSON NOW HAD NO INCOME.

BACK IN NINGBO HE HOPED TO SEE MARIA AGAIN, BUT THE HEAD TEACHER TRIED TO PREVENT THEM FROM BEING TOGETHER.

ONE DAY DURING A PRAYER MEETING, IT STARTED POURING WITH RAIN AND THE PLACE WAS COMPLETELY FLOODED.

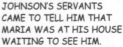

JOHNSON'S SERVANTS CAME TO TELL HIM THAT MARIA WAS AT HIS HOUSE WAITING TO SEE HIM.

JOHNSON THOUGHT THIS WOULD BE A GOOD OPPORTUNITY FOR HUDSON AND MARIA TO MEET, SO HE ASKED HUDSON TO GO BACK WITH HIM

AFTER SO MANY DIFFICULTIES, HUDSON AND MARIA FINALLY HAD AN OPPORTUNITY TO OPEN THEIR HEARTS TO EACH OTHER. THEY PRAYED TOGETHER, HOPING GOD WOULD PUT HIS HAND OVER THEM. HUDSON DECIDED TO WRITE TO MARIA'S GUARDIAN IN ENGLAND TO ASK FOR PERMISSION TO MARRY HER.

MY HEART IS QUIETLY WAITING FOR AN ANSWER FROM GOD. I KNOW THAT THOSE WHO FEAR HIM WILL NOT LACK ANYTHING.

THE GRACE OF THE LORD IS SO DEEP. IN NOVEMBER, MARIA'S GUARDIAN WROTE BACK, PRAISING HUDSON'S WORK AND GIVING HIS APPROVAL FOR THEIR MARRIAGE.

LONG AFTERWARDS, HUDSON WROTE, "WE SAT THERE, SHOULDER TO SHOULDER, HOLDING HANDS. MY LOVE FOR HER HAS NEVER GROWN COLD. IT HAS ALWAYS STAYED THE SAME."

MRS ELTON FROM THE AMERICAN SOUTHERN BAPTIST MISSION WAS HELPFUL AND KIND. SHE TOOK SPECIAL CARE OF THE YOUNG COUPLE.

SHE INVITED MARIA AND HUDSON TO HER HOME SO THEY COULD SPEND TIME TOGETHER.

A FEW DAYS BEFORE THE WEDDING.

"MARIA, YOU CAN SEE HOW FULL OF DIFFICULTIES MY LIFE IS. WOULD YOU RATHER CANCEL THE WEDDING?"

"GOD IS OUR FATHER. DON'T YOU REMEMBER? HOW WOULD A FATHER ABANDON HIS BELOVED CHILDREN? DO YOU THINK THAT WE CAN'T TRUST OUR FUTURE TO HIM?"

"WHO CAN FIND A CAPABLE WIFE? SHE IS FAR MORE PRECIOUS THAN JEWELS."

20TH JANUARY, 1858

THE WEDDING WAS HELD AT
THE BRITISH CONSULATE.
AFTER THE WEDDING, THEY
WENT TO THE WESTERN HILLS
FOR THEIR HONEYMOON.

"THE LORD HAS PUT US TOGETHER, SHOWERING HIS LOVE AND GRACE UPON US. WE FEEL WE COULDN'T BE HAPPIER THAN THIS!"

"WE WORK TOGETHER AND SUPPORT EACH OTHER, PREACHING, TREATING THE SICK AND VISITING FRIENDS."

BIBLE

BIBLE - NINGBO DIALECT VERSION

THE POOR PEOPLE COULD NOT READ, AND CHINESE IS A DIFFICULT LANGUAGE. HUDSON DEVELOPED AN ALPHABETICAL SYSTEM TO TEACH THEM THE BIBLE. IT WORKED VERY WELL, AND EVEN THE ELDERLY COULD READ IT.

THE TIAN JING TREATY WAS SIGNED BETWEEN THE BRITISH AND CHINESE GOVERNMENT. IT ALLOWED FOREIGNERS TO TRAVEL INTO CHINA'S INTERIOR.

16TH FEBRUARY, 1858

HUDSON LOVED TO PREACH TO THE PEOPLE. OFTEN THERE WAS AN OLD GRANNY AMONG THE LISTENERS, BRINGING HER GRANDSON TO MEET WITH THE LORD.

THE PEOPLE WERE OVERJOYED WHEN THEY HEARD THE GOOD NEWS AND WERE SAVED. THEY READ THE BIBLE AND SPREAD THE GOSPEL TO OTHERS.

ONE DAY MARIA FELL ILL. HUDSON TRIED EVERYTHING BUT HE COULDN'T MAKE HER BETTER. HE KNELT IN PRAYER.

ALL OF A SUDDEN, HE REMEMBERED PARKER. HE WENT STRAIGHT TO HIM FOR HELP

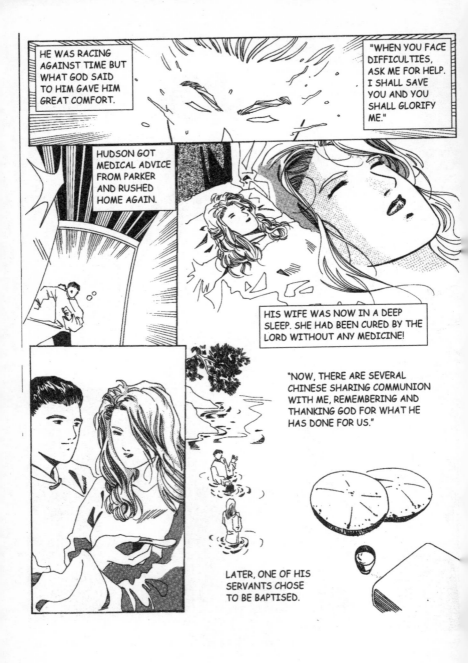

HE WAS RACING AGAINST TIME BUT WHAT GOD SAID TO HIM GAVE HIM GREAT COMFORT.

"WHEN YOU FACE DIFFICULTIES, ASK ME FOR HELP. I SHALL SAVE YOU AND YOU SHALL GLORIFY ME."

HUDSON GOT MEDICAL ADVICE FROM PARKER AND RUSHED HOME AGAIN.

HIS WIFE WAS NOW IN A DEEP SLEEP. SHE HAD BEEN CURED BY THE LORD WITHOUT ANY MEDICINE!

"NOW, THERE ARE SEVERAL CHINESE SHARING COMMUNION WITH ME, REMEMBERING AND THANKING GOD FOR WHAT HE HAS DONE FOR US."

LATER, ONE OF HIS SERVANTS CHOSE TO BE BAPTISED.

31ST JULY, 1859

"MUM AND DAD, I AM REALLY HAPPY. IT'S A PITY YOU'RE NOT IN CHINA WITH US."

"THIS IS SUCH A WONDERFUL GIFT FROM GOD, YOUR FIRST GRANDDAUGHTER. WE HAVE CALLED HER EN HUI (GRACE). SHE IS LOVELY. GOD IS GOOD TO US, AND WE HOLD HIS NAME HIGH."

AUGUST 1859

MRS PARKER DIED, LEAVING FOUR CHILDREN MOTHERLESS.

FOR THE SAKE OF THE CHILDREN, PARKER DECIDED TO GO HOME TO SCOTLAND. HE ASKED HUDSON TO TAKE OVER THE HOSPITAL. THE TAYLORS AGREED.

AFTER HUDSON TOOK OVER, THE HOSPITAL CONTINUED TO GROW.

HOWEVER, THE MONEY THAT PARKER LEFT WAS QUICKLY GONE.

IT IS TIME FOR GOD TO PROVIDE.

"DIRECTOR TAYLOR. A LETTER FOR YOU."

TWO BROTHERS HAD SENT A DONATION - EVEN THOUGH THEY DID NOT KNOW ABOUT THE NEED. WITH THIS BLESSING, THE HOSPITAL HAD ENOUGH MONEY FOR THE COMING DAYS. IT COULD GO ON TREATING THE POOR. WITHIN MONTHS, SIXTEEN PEOPLE WERE BAPTISED. THERE WERE NOW THIRTY BELIEVERS IN NINGBO AND OVER SIX HUNDRED PEOPLE WHO HAD BEEN TO THE HOSPITAL HAD ALL HEARD THE GOSPEL.

NINGBO CHRISTIAN TRUST HOPE AND LOVE CHURCH

EVERYONE HAS TO BEAR HIS OWN CROSS.

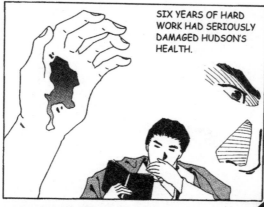

SIX YEARS OF HARD WORK HAD SERIOUSLY DAMAGED HUDSON'S HEALTH.

SUMMER 1860

EVERYONE AGREED THAT HUDSON NEEDED TO GO BACK TO THE UK FOR SOME MEDICAL ATTENTION AND REST. THEY HAD TO STOP THE WORK IN THE HOSPITAL. FINALLY, WITH GOD'S HELP, HUDSON AND MARIA GOT ON THE BOAT BACK TO ENGLAND.

"GOD WANTS TO SAVE THE CHINESE, AND HE HAS ALREADY BLESSED OUR WORK. BUT WE ARE EXHAUSTED AND NEED HELP. CHINA IS A HUGE COUNTRY, AND WE FEEL SO SMALL AND VULNERABLE. I HOPE THAT THE CHURCHES IN THE UK WILL UNDERSTAND OUR OBLIGATION TO PREACH THE GOSPEL IN CHINA. GOD KNOWS OUR NEEDS AND HE WILL PROVIDE. IF I HAD A THOUSAND POUNDS, CHINA COULD TAKE IT ALL. IF I HAD A THOUSAND LIVES, I WOULDN'T KEEP A SINGLE ONE, BUT GIVE THEM ALL TO CHINA. DO YOU TRUST IN GOD? COULD YOU DO A GREAT JOB FOR HIM?"

BACK IN ENGLAND HUDSON PREACHED AND WROTE LETTERS, URGING MORE PEOPLE TO GO TO WORK IN CHINA.

Total Love

Hudson aged 28–38

WHILE HE WAS RESTING IN THE UK, HUDSON CONTINUED TO WORK.

HE RENTED A HOUSE IN LONDON AND FINISHED HIS MEDICAL STUDIES. THEN HE EDITED THE BIBLE IN THE NINGBO DIALECT, GETTING IT READY FOR PUBLICATION.

HUDSON PERSUADED THE CHAIRMAN TO LET HIM SPEAK AT THE 3RD SCOTTISH CHRISTIAN CONFERENCE.

SEPTEMBER 1864

HIS SPEECH WAS FULL OF HIS TRUST IN GOD'S LOVE, FAITHFULNESS AND POWER. THE AUDIENCE LISTENED INTENTLY.

THEY FINALLY CAME AND PETER WAS PULLED OUT, BUT BECAUSE OF THESE HEARTLESS FISHERMEN IT WAS TOO LATE. A LIFE WAS LOST WHEN IT COULD EASILY HAVE BEEN SAVED.

WE CAN'T BELIEVE THESE PEOPLE ARE SO APATHETIC! I COULD SAY THAT THESE FISHERMEN ARE GUILTY, AND BLAME THEM FOR MURDERING PETER. BUT ISN'T THE SOUL MORE IMPORTANT THAN THE BODY? AND WE KNOW THAT HUNDREDS OF THOUSANDS OF PEOPLE DIE EVERY DAY WITH THEIR SOULS UNSAVED. IF WE DO NOTHING TO SAVE THEM, WE ARE AS GUILTY AS THOSE FISHERMEN.

GOD SAID, "GO INTO ALL THE WORLD AND PREACH THE GOOD NEWS TO ALL CREATION". HAVE WE DONE THAT YET?

YOU MAY SAY, "I DIDN'T SENSE ANY SPECIAL CALLING FROM GOD". BUT YOU'RE WRONG. YOU SHOULD ASK YOURSELF RATHER WHETHER GOD HAS CALLED YOU TO STAY AT HOME. NO? THEN WHY DON'T YOU FOLLOW GOD'S COMMAND TO PREACH THE GOOD NEWS? HAVE YOU DONE YOUR BEST? HAVE YOU OFFERED YOUR TIME AND MONEY AND PRAYER FOR LOST SOULS?

GOD HAS WALKED IN FRONT AND PAVED THE WAY FOR US TO PREACH THE GOSPEL IN CHINA. CAN WE SAY TO GOD THAT IT'S "NOT CONVENIENT", BECAUSE WE'RE BUSY FISHING, OR DOING SOMETHING ELSE? REMEMBER, EVERYONE HAS TO SHOW WHAT WE'VE DONE IN FRONT OF OUR LORD. PLEASE PRAY FOR THOSE IN CHINA WHO HAVE NEVER HEARD THE GOSPEL.

AT THE END OF HUDSON'S SPEECH THE PEOPLE WERE STUNNED. MANY OF THEM CAME TO OFFER THEIR SUPPORT FOR HIS WORK.

HUDSON LOOKED BACK OVER WHAT HE HAD ACHIEVED. STUDYING THE MAP OF CHINA, HE SAW THAT HIS WORK HAD ONLY CONCENTRATED ON THE NEEDS OF NINGBO. HE REALISED HE HAD NEGLECTED OTHER MORE IMPORTANT PROBLEMS. THERE WAS SO MUCH NEED... HE PUT THOSE NEEDS INTO GOD'S HANDS. ISN'T GOD TRUSTWORTHY?

CHINA

IN OCTOBER 1864, HUDSON SENT THREE MORE MISSIONARIES TO CHINA, TO ASSIST THE MISSIONARY WORK IN NINGBO.

JUNE 1865

TODAY IS SUNDAY.

"I VISITED SOME FRIENDS AND WORSHIPPED WITH THEM. I WAS FEELING PHYSICALLY EXHAUSTED, BUT SEEING THE BELIEVERS' JOY AND HAPPINESS... I ONCE AGAIN REMEMBERED THE URGENT NEEDS OF CHINA..."

"GOD PREPARES OUR WORKERS TO PREACH IN CHINA. THEY MAY DIE OF HUNGER OR SICKNESS, BUT IF SO, THEY WILL GO STRAIGHT TO HEAVEN. IF THEY MANAGE TO SAVE EVEN ONE SOUL, THEN THEIR SACRIFICE IS WORTHWHILE. NO MATTER HOW TRAGIC THE RESULT, IT'S STILL WORTH THE RISK."

"BESIDES, WE OBEY GOD. GOD, NOT US, WILL TAKE THE RESPONSIBILITY. WE'RE HIS SERVANTS. WE GO FORWARD ACCORDING TO HIS COMMANDS. HE DETERMINES THE END RESULT."

ON 27TH JUNE 1865, HUDSON AND PEARSE OPENED AN ACCOUNT IN A LONDON BANK FOR MAINLAND CHINA.

STOTT

MRS HUDSON TAYLOR

FOUR OF THEM CO-OPERATED TO EDIT HUDSON'S BOOK, CALLED *SPIRITUAL NEEDS AND DEMANDS IN CHINA*...

STEVENSON

WHEN I THINK OF THE GREAT AND URGENT NEEDS IN CHINA, AND LOOK BACK TO THOSE WHO ARE WILLING TO SERVE, IT WORRIES ME DEEPLY. THE CAPABLE PEOPLE DO NOT WANT TO LEAD, AND WORDS FROM THOSE OF LOWLY POSITION CARRY LITTLE WEIGHT. THIS IS SHAMEFUL FOR CHRISTIANS, AND WE'RE GUILTY OF NEGLECTING OUR DUTY. GOD SAID,

"SURELY THE ARM OF THE LORD IS NOT TOO SHORT TO SAVE, NOR HIS EAR TOO DULL TO HEAR." "ASK AND YOU WILL RECEIVE, AND YOUR JOY WILL BE COMPLETE."

WE HAVE RECEIVED A GREAT RESPONSIBILITY FROM GOD, AND ENORMOUS ENCOURAGEMENT AND PROMISES FROM HIS WORD. WE CAN CALL FOR GOD'S HELP WITHOUT HESITATION. WE PRAY THAT HE WILL SEND 24 BRITISH AND CHINESE COLLEAGUES TO 11 PROVINCES AND INNER MONGOLIA WHERE PEOPLE HAVE NEVER HEARD OF THE GOSPEL, AND ESTABLISH THE FLAG OF JESUS CHRIST THERE. THESE VENTURES MAY BE DANGEROUS BUT WE CAN TESTIFY TO GOD'S TRUSTWORTHINESS. NO MATTER HOW DIFFICULT IT IS, HE WILL HELP US. IN BYGONE DAYS, I PERSONALLY EXPERIENCED GOD'S HELP, PROVISION AND CARE CONTINUOUSLY AND SUFFICIENTLY. IN THE PAST EIGHT YEARS, THERE HAVE BEEN NO MISHAPS.

"SEEK YE FIRST THE KINGDOM OF GOD AND HIS RIGHTEOUSNESS, AND ALL THESE THINGS WILL BE ADDED UNTO YOU."

WHAT ARE THESE THINGS? EVERYTHING IN THE WORLD BELONGS TO GOD. "NO GOOD THING DOES HE WITHHOLD FROM THOSE WHOSE WALK IS BLAMELESS."

GOD'S WORDS ARE FULL OF POWER AND PROMISES. IF YOU DON'T BELIEVE HIS WORDS, DON'T GO TO PREACH IN CHINA. IF YOU BELIEVE, SURELY YOU'LL SEE THE GLORY AND PROMISE OF GOD. IN THE PAST GOD SUPPORTED 3 MILLION ISRAELITES IN THE WILDERNESS FOR 40 YEARS, SO HE WILL ALSO PROVIDE AND CARE FOR HIS CHILDREN NOWADAYS. I DARE NOT HOPE THAT GOD WILL SEND 3 MILLION MISSIONARIES TO CHINA. HOWEVER, IF IT IS GOD'S WILL, HE WILL PROVIDE . IF WE WORK SPIRITUALLY, GOD'S HELP WILL BE SUFFICIENT.

THE TIANJING TREATY OF 1858 ALLOWED FOREIGNERS TO ENTER CHINA'S BORDERS. WE ORIGINALLY THOUGHT THAT IT WOULD BE DIFFICULT TO PREACH IN CHINA, BUT WITH GOD'S GUIDANCE, THE PATHWAY TO CHINA HAS BEEN OPENED. "ALL AUTHORITY IN HEAVEN AND ON EARTH HAS BEEN GIVEN TO ME."

NOW GOD CALLS US TO GLORIFY HIM BY SAVING THE LOST SOULS. LET'S OBEY HIS COMMAND. DESPITE THE DANGERS AHEAD, CHRIST IS OUR LORD. WE CAN FOLLOW HIM IN PEACE AND DEPEND ON HIM IN OUR WEAKNESS. THEN EVEN THE WEAKEST SERVANT CAN BE FILLED WITH GOD'S BLESSING AND COME BACK VICTORIOUS.

"IN THIS WORLD YOU WILL HAVE TROUBLE. BUT TAKE HEART! I HAVE OVERCOME THE WORLD."
GOD MUST BE WITH US. THIS IS THE TIME TO SHOW OUR FAITH TOWARDS HIM. WE SHOULD NOT WORRY. GOD IS TRUSTWORTHY.

"THOSE WHO KNOW YOUR NAME WILL TRUST IN YOU."

HUDSON'S BOOK WAS PUBLISHED BY PARKER AND DISTRIBUTED IN DIFFERENT COUNTRIES. IT SOLD OUT AND HAD TO BE REPRINTED.

SPIRITUAL NEEDS AND DEMANDS IN CHINA

HUDSON WANTED TO GATHER CHURCH WORKERS FROM DIFFERENT PLACES TO TAKE PART IN A MIGHTY WORK IN CHINA. HE KNEW THAT HE ALONE COULD NOT RECRUIT TEAM MEMBERS WHO WERE SPIRITUALLY SOUND, SO HE PRAYED FOR GOD'S PROVISION AND CALLING. "WE NEED TO BUILD UP OUR CHRISTIAN LIVES TO WORK FOR GOD. THROUGH THE HOLY SPIRIT CHRISTIANS CAN HAVE A DEEPER RELATIONSHIP WITH GOD, LEARN TO FOLLOW HIS WILL, TO RELY ON AND GLORIFY HIM."

HUDSON BELIEVED COMPLETELY IN GOD'S SOVEREIGN POWER. HE PRAYED THAT GOD WOULD PROVIDE ENOUGH FUNDING TO PAY THE EXPENSES FOR 22 MISSIONARIES. IN THE FIRST MONTH, £170 WAS GIVEN TO HIS FUND FOR MAINLAND CHINA. IN THE SECOND MONTH, £2,000. HUDSON KNEW THAT GOD WOULD DELIVER EVERYTHING THAT WAS NEEDED TO COMPLETE THE WORK HE WANTED THEM TO DO.

"TREES ARE VERY SIMILAR TO CHURCHES. AT THE BEGINNING, WE CAN SEE ONLY A SMALL SEEDLING WITH A FEW BUDS. BUT THEN IT STARTS TO GROW BRANCHES AND LATER BECOMES A BIG TREE. THE POINT IS THAT THOSE WHO PLANT THE TREE MUST WAIT AND BE PATIENT. ONCE THERE IS A LIFE, IT WILL GROW."

IN MAY 1866, THEY SAILED TO CHINA.

SO STUPID AND IGNORANT. THEY'RE GOING TO STARVE.

NON-BELIEVERS LAUGHED AT THEM FOR SETTING OFF INTO THE UNKNOWN. THERE WERE 22 PEOPLE ALTOGETHER, MEN AND WOMEN, ADULTS AND CHILDREN. HUDSON IGNORED THE CRITICISM.

MOST OF THE SAILORS ON BOARD WERE NON-BELIEVERS. HOWEVER, THEY WERE IMPRESSED BY THE HELPFUL, KINDLY CHRISTIANS WHO EAGERLY SHARED THE GOSPEL, AND MANY OF THE SAILORS AND OFFICERS TURNED TO GOD. DESPITE SATAN'S ATTACKS, GOD ALWAYS GAINS THE FINAL VICTORY. AFTER A FOUR-MONTH JOURNEY, THEY ARRIVED SAFELY IN SHANGHAI.

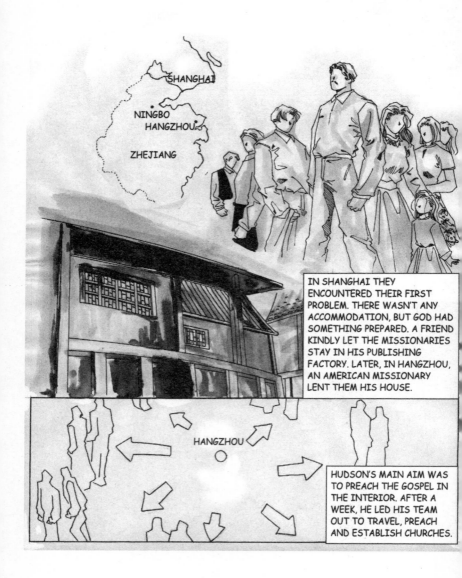

SHANGHAI

NINGBO
HANGZHOU

ZHEJIANG

IN SHANGHAI THEY
ENCOUNTERED THEIR FIRST
PROBLEM. THERE WASN'T ANY
ACCOMMODATION, BUT GOD HAD
SOMETHING PREPARED. A FRIEND
KINDLY LET THE MISSIONARIES
STAY IN HIS PUBLISHING
FACTORY. LATER, IN HANGZHOU,
AN AMERICAN MISSIONARY
LENT THEM HIS HOUSE.

HANGZHOU

HUDSON'S MAIN AIM WAS
TO PREACH THE GOSPEL IN
THE INTERIOR. AFTER A
WEEK, HE LED HIS TEAM
OUT TO TRAVEL, PREACH
AND ESTABLISH CHURCHES.

A CHURCH AND CLINIC WERE OPENED IN HANGZHOU, AND OVER 200 PEOPLE CAME TO WORSHIP OR CONSULT DOCTORS.

"DID I NOT TELL YOU THAT IF YOU BELIEVED, YOU WOULD SEE THE GLORY OF GOD?" (JOHN 11:40)

IN AUGUST 1867, HUDSON'S DIARY WAS FILLED WITH TEARS.

GRACE, HIS 8-YEAR-OLD DAUGHTER, CAUGHT MENINGITIS WHILST STAYING AT A SUMMER RESORT.

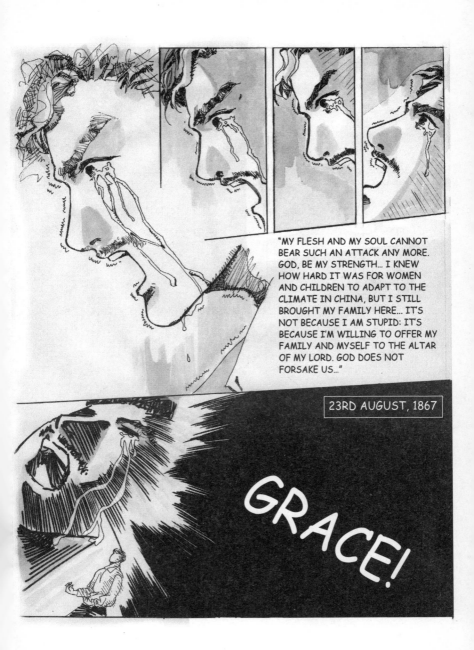

"MY FLESH AND MY SOUL CANNOT BEAR SUCH AN ATTACK ANY MORE. GOD, BE MY STRENGTH... I KNEW HOW HARD IT WAS FOR WOMEN AND CHILDREN TO ADAPT TO THE CLIMATE IN CHINA, BUT I STILL BROUGHT MY FAMILY HERE... IT'S NOT BECAUSE I AM STUPID: IT'S BECAUSE I'M WILLING TO OFFER MY FAMILY AND MYSELF TO THE ALTAR OF MY LORD. GOD DOES NOT FORSAKE US..."

23RD AUGUST, 1867

GRACE!

"HER WARMTH AND LIFE HAVE GROWN COLD AND STILL. I'LL NEVER HEAR HER JOYFUL LAUGH AGAIN, OR SEE HER LOVELY FACE... BUT SHE STILL LIVES IN MY MEMORY, THANK GOD."

"SHE HAS GONE TO BE WITH CHRIST - IN A HOLY, HAPPY PLACE. HEAVEN IS BETTER THAN THIS WORLD. I WOULD NOT ASK TO HAVE HER BACK. WHO PICKED THIS BEAUTIFUL FLOWER? THE MASTER PICKED IT."

THE CHURCH HAD SPREAD INTO DIFFERENT PARTS OF CHINA. CHINESE LADIES WERE ESPECIALLY EAGER TO HEAR THE GOOD NEWS. MORE AND MORE PEOPLE ATTENDED CHURCH, AND LARGE NUMBERS WERE BAPTISED.

HOWEVER, BELIEVERS WERE OFTEN THROWN INTO JAIL, CRUELLY BEATEN OR EXPELLED. "SATAN WAS ATTACKING US FIERCELY. FINALLY, WE SHIFTED OUR MISSIONARY WORK TO THE NORTH."

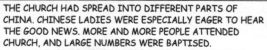

JIASHAN

JIAXING

HANGZHOU

FENGHUA

JINHUA

YONG KANG

LISHUI

JIULONG

WENZHOU

YANGZHOU

IN THE SUMMER OF 1868, HUDSON TAYLOR WENT TO WORK IN YANGZHOU, WHERE MANY CHILDREN WERE SICK. MRS TAYLOR HURRIED TO YANGZHOU TO TAKE CARE OF THEM.

IN AUGUST THERE WAS TROUBLE. THE PEOPLE IN YANGZHOU PROTESTED ABOUT THE FOREIGNERS STAYING THERE.

THEY CLAIMED THAT THEY WERE STEALING CHINESE CHILDREN. A MOB GATHERED TO ATTACK THEM.

MARIA HAD TO JUMP FROM THE SECOND FLOOR, AND SERIOUSLY INJURED HER LEG. THE SITUATION WAS STEADILY GROWING MORE DANGEROUS.

MISSIONARY REID WAS HIT IN THE EYE WITH A STONE.

POLICE OFFICERS ARRIVED TO DISPERSE THE MOB.

THEY FOUND THAT THE RIOTERS HAD SET FIRE TO THE HOUSE. FORTUNATELY TAYLOR AND THE OTHERS ESCAPED.

IN THE END THEY HAD TO LEAVE YANGZHOU AND RETURN TO ZHENJIANG. THEY LEFT EVERYTHING BEHIND, AND BY GOD'S GRACE THEIR MONEY AND DOCUMENTS WERE NOT STOLEN.

HUDSON!

HUDSON AND MARIA WEPT TOGETHER. THEY WERE SO THANKFUL TO GOD FOR SPARING THEIR LIVES.

WHO IS IT?

THE SHANGHAI DAILY NEWSPAPERS REPORTED THE WHOLE STORY, WHICH ANGERED THE BRITISH EMBASSY. BRITISH OFFICIALS PROTESTED AT THEIR TREATMENT, BUT HUDSON WAS SAD. HE WISHED THEY COULD STOP THE OFFICIALS FROM TAKING ACTION. IT WOULD BE BETTER TO RETURN GOOD FOR EVIL, TO SHOW THE CHINESE A BETTER WAY.

THEN SATAN BEGAN TO TURN HUDSON'S COLLEAGUES AGAINST HIM. THEY BLAMED HIM AND HIS STYLE OF LEADERSHIP FOR ALL THEIR TROUBLES.

HUDSON AND MARIA DID NOT ARGUE. THEY SIMPLY ASKED THOSE PEOPLE TO LEAVE. SEVERAL OTHER COLLEAGUES ALSO RESIGNED.

"TO WORK TOGETHER WE MUST SHARE THE SAME GOAL. YOU NEED TO BE EAGER TO GET TO KNOW THE CHINESE AND LEARN THEIR LANGUAGE, AND WILLING TO LIVE FAR FROM YOUR OWN FAMILY. IF YOU'RE NOT WILLING TO MAKE THESE SACRIFICES, PLEASE DON'T JOIN US. WE NEED THE STRENGTH TO BEAR EVERY BURDEN AND FRUSTRATION, FOR THE SAKE OF JESUS CHRIST, FOR CHINA AND FOR THOSE PRECIOUS SOULS."

LONDON, NOVEMBER 1868. PARLIAMENT DISCUSSED THE ISSUE OF MISSIONARY WORK IN MAINLAND CHINA. SOME MEMBERS WERE VERY CRITICAL OF HUDSON TAYLOR, AND WANTED ALL THE BRITISH MISSIONARIES TO LEAVE CHINA. AS A RESULT, OFFERINGS TO THE MISSION WERE GREATLY REDUCED.

THERE SEEMED TO BE NO END TO THE DIFFICULTIES AND ATTACKS ON THE MISSIONARY WORK.

HUDSON WAS ALMOST OVERWHELMED. THE MOST TRAGIC THING FOR HIM WAS TO LOSE HIS CLOSE RELATIONSHIP WITH GOD.

DEAR MUM,
PLEASE PRAY FOR ME. I FEEL THAT I'M CONSTANTLY UNDER ATTACK FROM BOTH INSIDE AND OUTSIDE THE MISSION. I DON'T KNOW WHETHER TO GO FORWARD OR RETREAT, AND I'M SO WEARY. BUT I KNOW I'M DOING GOD'S WORK AND HE IS WITH ME. GOD WILL DECIDE THE END RESULT. I'M ASHAMED TO FEEL SO DEFEATED: MY HEART IS WEAK AND I KNOW I DON'T LOVE HIM ENOUGH. I NEED MORE GRACE FROM GOD TO DO HIS WILL AND SERVE HIM WITH FAITH.
JESUS IS THE MOST PRECIOUS THING IN MY LIFE, AND I SHOULD LOVE HIM MORE. I HOPE GOD WILL HELP ME. PLEASE PRAY FOR ME.
HUDSON,
13TH MARCH, 1869

IN SEPTEMBER, MISSIONARY MAK SENT HIM A LETTER ...

101

MR TAYLOR

I HAVE BEEN THINKING HARD ABOUT HOLY LIVING. I OFTEN THINK I'M A FAILURE: I SEEK A DEEPER RELATIONSHIP WITH GOD, BUT WORKING HARDER OR JUST HOPING DOES NOT WORK. I STRUGGLE AND WORRY AND FAIL OVER AND OVER AGAIN. ALL THESE PROBLEMS PROVE THAT I AM NOT LIVING A HOLY LIFE.

WHAT IS THE SECRET? RECEIVING JESUS CHRIST IS THE BEGINNING OF HAVING A HOLY LIFE. STAYING CLOSE TO GOD IS PROGRESS TOWARDS A HOLY LIFE. WALKING WITH HIM EVERY DAY IS THE WAY TO ACHIEVE A HOLY LIFE. OUR FAITH IS A KIND OF TRAINING IN HOLINESS, AND IT IS AN UNFAITHFUL HEART WHICH MAKES US STUMBLE.

SO I AM TRYING TO LIFT UP MY EYES TO GOD. I TURN AWAY FROM MY OWN SIN AND FAILURE, BECAUSE I KNOW JESUS HAS DIED TO SET ME FREE FROM THAT. I CAN GIVE UP STRUGGLING AND I CAN REST IN PEACE. TO BECOME HOLY, ALL I NEED IS TO THINK ABOUT JESUS - HIS LIFE, HIS WORK, HIS DEATH, AND HIS WORD. I DON'T ASK FOR MORE TRUST IN HIM, BUT TO LIFT HIM UP ON HIGH. THAT IS ENOUGH.

ONE OF OUR SISTERS IN THE MISSION WROTE TO ME RECENTLY AND SAID, "I, TOO, HAVE STRUGGLED IN MY MISSIONARY WORK. MY HEAVY WORKLOAD, MY PHYSICAL WEAKNESSES, THE CLIMATE, MY WAY OF THINKING AND THE LANGUAGE ALL SEEMED TO BE BURDENS FOR ME TO BEAR. AGAIN AND AGAIN I FORGOT ABOUT GOD AND SINNED AGAINST HIM. I PRAYED, REPENTED, FASTED AND MEDITATED, YET I STILL FELT VERY WEAK SPIRITUALLY.

THANK GOD, I CAME TO UNDERSTAND WHY I'M POOR AND DON'T GET HIS STRENGTH. I SIMPLY NEED TO TRUST, TO STRETCH OUT MY HANDS AND ACCEPT HIS RICHES. HARD WORK CANNOT GAIN TRUST; THE ONLY WAY IS TO DEPEND ON HIM. NOW THE LORD HAS TAKEN ALL MY BURDENS. I WAS BLIND BUT NOW I CAN SEE. I'M SO JOYFUL, BECAUSE I DON'T HAVE TO STRIVE ANY LONGER, JUST REST IN HIS LOVE."

"IF WE ARE FAITHLESS, HE WILL REMAIN FAITHFUL." (2 TIMOTHY 2:13)

"THIS IS THE CONFIDENCE WE HAVE IN APPROACHING GOD: THAT IF WE ASK ANYTHING ACCORDING TO HIS WILL, HE HEARS US. AND IF WE KNOW THAT HE HEARS US - WHATEVER WE ASK - WE KNOW THAT WE HAVE WHAT WE ASKED OF HIM." (1 JOHN 5:14-15)

"WHOEVER DRINKS THE WATER I GIVE HIM WILL NEVER THIRST." (JOHN 4:14)

THAT LETTER SPOKE TO HUDSON'S HEART AND BROUGHT HIM INTO A NEW UNDERSTANDING OF GOD'S GRACE. HE REALISED THAT HE COULD NOT DO GOD'S WORK IN HIS OWN STRENGTH. INSTEAD HE HAD TO TRUST IN THE PROMISES OF JESUS.

"I WILL NEVER FAIL YOU NOR FORSAKE YOU." (HEBREWS 13:5) HE KNEW THAT GOD'S STRENGTH WAS ALWAYS SUFFICIENT.

"I HAVE BEEN CRUCIFIED WITH CHRIST AND I NO LONGER LIVE, BUT CHRIST LIVES IN ME." (GALATIANS 2:20) HE WENT FORWARD WITH NEW HOPE.

HYMNS OF PRAISE

IN 1870 HUDSON WENT BACK TO HIS WORK WITH NEW STRENGTH. HE CARED FOR THE CHINESE WHO WORKED ALONGSIDE HIM.

HE KNEW THAT MR JOK'S HEALTH WAS POOR, SO HE ARRANGED TO BUY A PONY. EVERYONE THOUGHT IT WAS FOR HUDSON'S USE, BUT SOMEHOW HE NEVER FOUND TIME TO RIDE IT. HE ASKED MR JOK TO CARE FOR THE PONY AND EXERCISE IT, SO MR JOK WAS ABLE TO RIDE WHEN HE WENT OUT TO PREACH. HUDSON OFTEN HELPED OTHERS SECRETLY IN THIS WAY, WITHOUT ASKING FOR THANKS.

THE CHILDREN WERE GROWING UP, BUT FIVE-YEAR-OLD SAMUEL WAS ILL.

THE TAYLORS KNEW THE CHILDREN WOULD HAVE BETTER HEALTH IN ENGLAND, SO THEY ARRANGED FOR THEM TO GO HOME.

THEY SET OFF ACROSS THE YANGZI RIVER TO TAKE THE CHILDREN TO SHANGHAI.

SAMUEL'S ILLNESS GOT WORSE, AND HE DIED.

FOREVER IN PEACE...

H JULY. "WE REJOICED
HEN MARIA GAVE BIRTH TO A
BY BOY. BUT SHE WAS VERY
..., AND SO WAS THE BABY.
HEY BOTH GREW WEAKER,
ND AFTER A WEEK, OUR CHILD
TURNED TO THE LORD."

23RD JULY.
"MY WIFE
WAS ILL. SHE
CALLED OUT
TO ME ..."

HUDSON!

"HER FACE WAS PALE ... SHE LOOKED
AS THOUGH SHE WAS ALREADY DEAD."

MY BELOVED WIFI ... YOU WILL SEE OUR CHILDREN IN HEAVEN.

HUDSON... IT WON'T BE LONG NOW.

MY DEAR, ARE YOU IN PAIN?

NO ... I DON'T FEEL ... PAIN, I'M ONLY ... TIRED.

BE AT PEACE ... YOU'RE GOING TO GO TO BE WITH JESUS CHRIST.

BUT I'M WORRIED ...

WHY ARE YOU AFRAID? YOU'RE GOING TO BE WITH JESUS.

NO... THAT'S NOT WHAT I MEAN. THE LORD HAS ALWAYS LOVED AND CARED FOR US. I'M HAPPY TO SEE HIM. BUT... I HATE TO LEAVE YOU... TO BEAR EVERY BURDEN BY YOURSELF... I PRAY THAT GOD WILL BE WITH YOU... FOR EVER...

ON 23RD JULY, MARIA TAYLOR WENT TO BE WITH GOD. HUDSON KNELT BESIDE HER AND THANKED GOD FOR HIS WIFE OF MORE THAN 10 YEARS. HE ACCEPTED THAT SHE HAD GONE HOME TO JESUS.

ON 4TH AUGUST, HUDSON WROTE IN A LETTER:

GOD KNOWS HOW MUCH I LOVED MY WIFE, YET HE HAS TAKEN HER AND LEFT ME TO WORK ALONE. I KNOW HE IS CALLING ME TO BE CLOSER TO HIM. THOUGH I CAN NO LONGER PRAY WITH MARIA, I KNOW THAT JESUS IS ALIVE AND PRAYING FOR US. HE CAN LEAD ME OUT OF SORROW AND GIVE ME COMFORT.

HUDSON WAS FACING A HARSH AND LONELY PERIOD OF HIS LIFE. HIS FAMILY HAD BEEN BROKEN UP, HIS FRIENDS HAD LEFT HIM, AND HIS OWN HEALTH WAS NOT GOOD. COULD GOD SATISFY HIS SPIRITUAL NEEDS?

ON 18 NOVEMBER HUDSON WROTE:
   THANK YOU FOR YOUR CARE AND CONSOLATION. MY WIFE HAS GONE FROM ME
PHYSICALLY, BUT I DO NOT FEEL THAT SHE HAS GONE AWAY. OUR LOVE HAS NEVER
CHANGED, AND OUR HEARTS HAVE NEVER BEEN APART. I FEEL I UNDERSTAND GOD'S
WISDOM AND KINDNESS MORE DEEPLY.
   "I AM THE BREAD OF LIFE. HE WHO COMES TO ME WILL NEVER GO HUNGRY, AND HE
WHO BELIEVES IN ME WILL NEVER BE THIRSTY." (JOHN 6:35) GOD HAS GIVEN US A LIVING
FOUNTAIN. HE DOESN'T WANT US TO BE SATISFIED WITH ONLY A SIP, BUT TO DRINK THE
FOUNTAIN WATER FREQUENTLY, SO OUR FAITH IN HIM WILL GROW.

Come on, brothers and sisters!

Hudson aged 39–61

HUDSON WENT HOME TO LONDON AND MET UP WITH HIS OLD FRIEND PARKER.

MARCH 1872

PARKER WAS GROWING OLD AND WAS READY TO RETIRE. AS THE BRITISH MISSIONARY ASSOCIATION'S REPRESENTATIVE IN MAINLAND CHINA, HE PASSED HIS WORK ON TO HUDSON.

JENNY

ON THE LONG JOURNEY TO ENGLAND, HUDSON HAD MET JENNY FAULDING. THE SEEDS OF LOVE WERE SOWN, AND LATER SHE BECAME THE SECOND MRS HUDSON TAYLOR.

RICHARD HILL

H. SOLTAU

EVEN IN BRITAIN HUDSON'S WORKLOAD WAS HEAVY, AND HE WAS STILL PHYSICALLY WEAK. A FRIEND WROTE AND REMINDED HIM OF MOSES AND JETHRO: "SELECT CAPABLE MEN... TO MAKE YOUR LOAD LIGHTER." (EXODUS 18:17-23)

THOSE WHO WISH TO WORK IN CHINA MUST HAVE A HEART TO LOVE SINNERS. THEY MUST BE TOUGH, ENERGETIC AND PREPARED TO WORK HARD.

IN AUGUST, HUDSON AND RICHARD HILL WORKED TOGETHER TO SET UP A CONSULTATION COMMITTEE TO SELECT MISSIONARIES. AT THE SAME TIME THEY STARTED A MISSIONARY TRAINING COURSE, CALLED "THE SCHOOL OF THE LAMB AND FLAG".

LATER THAT YEAR HUDSON WENT BACK TO SHANGHAI. HE FOUND THAT PROBLEMS WERE MOUNTING. SOME CHURCH LEADERS HAD DIED AND OTHERS HAD MOVED AWAY. NO ONE WAS SUPERVISING THE CHURCHES AND THE PEOPLE WERE DRIFTING AWAY FROM THE GOSPEL.

HUDSON HUMBLED HIMSELF BEFORE GOD. HE COULD NOT BLAME THE BELIEVERS: THEY HAD NO TEACHING. INSTEAD HE WAS SYMPATHETIC.

YANGZHOU

ZHENJIANG
NANJING

YELLOW
RIVER

HE SET OUT TO VISIT EVERY CHURCH IN THE AREA. THE MEMBERS WERE DELIGHTED AND EXCITED TO SEE THEIR FAMOUS LEADER, AND ALL THE CHURCHES WERE ENCOURAGED. MANY OTHER BUILDINGS, LIKE CASINOS AND NIGHTCLUBS, WERE TURNED INTO PLACES OF TEACHING AND WORSHIP.

REVEREND TAYLOR!
REVEREND TAYLOR!

"I DO HOPE THE GOSPEL CAN BE PREACHED TO THE MOST DISTANT AND ISOLATED PROVINCES IN CHINA."

IN JANUARY 1873 HUDSON WROTE:
PLEASE PRAY FOR ME EVERY DAY, THAT GOD WILL DIRECT ME TO THE PROVINCES I SHOULD VISIT. WE NEED 50 OR 100 CHINESE MISSIONARIES AS WELL AS SOME FOREIGN SUPERVISORS, TO WORK IN NEW PLACES IN ZHEJIANG. PLEASE ASK GOD TO SEND WORKERS TO THE NINE OTHER PROVINCES. IN JESUS' NAME, AMEN."

ONCE AGAIN HUDSON WAS SICK, BUT HE WAS CHEERED BY A LETTER OFFERING A GIFT OF £800. IT HAD BEEN SENT IN DECEMBER 1873 FOR THE PIONEERING MISSIONARY WORK IN MAINLAND CHINA. HE TOOK IT AS PROOF OF GOD'S PROVISION, AND CONTINUED TO PRAY AND ASK GOD FOR MORE.

TAIZHOU, JANUARY 1874.

HUBEI PROVINCE

IN JUNE 1874, MR ZHU RETURNED TO CHINA FROM BRITAIN. HUDSON WENT WITH HIM TO WUCHANG TO PREACH.

UNFORTUNATELY, HUDSON FELL DOWN SOME STEPS ON A BOAT, SERIOUSLY INJURING HIMSELF. FOR SEVERAL DAYS IT WAS TOO PAINFUL FOR HIM TO MOVE.

AH!

HIS ANKLE WAS SPRAINED AND HIS LOWER LEGS WERE TEMPORARILY PARALYSED: HE WAS CONFINED TO BED. ANYONE ELSE WOULD HAVE VIEWED THIS AS A DISASTER. HOWEVER, HUDSON ACCEPTED IT AS GOD'S WILL, AND AN OPPORTUNITY TO SPEND TIME IN PRAYER.

HE DECIDED TO RETURN TO BRITAIN.

IN EARLY 1875, HUDSON WAS STILL SICK IN BED. HE WROTE A LEAFLET ASKING HIS COLLEAGUES TO PRAY FOR AN HOUR EVERY DAY FOR THE PREACHING WORK IN CHINA AND THE NEEDS OF THE MISSIONARIES. HE ALSO ASKED GOD TO SEND 18 SUITABLE WORKERS TO BE LIGHT AND SALT IN CHINA. A GIFT OF £4,000 WAS GIVEN ANONYMOUSLY FOR THE WORK OF THE MISSION.

IN APRIL 1875, HUDSON SENT A LETTER TO THE MAINLAND. HE WAS RECOVERING AND BEGINNING TO WALK AGAIN. BUT HIS ENFORCED REST HAD GIVEN HIM TIME TO PLAN CAREFULLY THE BEST WAY OF PREACHING THE GOSPEL THROUGHOUT CHINA.

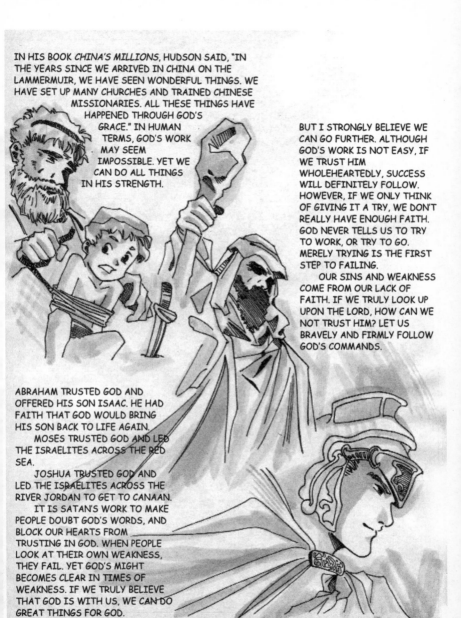

IN HIS BOOK *CHINA'S MILLIONS*, HUDSON SAID, "IN THE YEARS SINCE WE ARRIVED IN CHINA ON THE LAMMERMUIR, WE HAVE SEEN WONDERFUL THINGS. WE HAVE SET UP MANY CHURCHES AND TRAINED CHINESE MISSIONARIES. ALL THESE THINGS HAVE HAPPENED THROUGH GOD'S GRACE." IN HUMAN TERMS, GOD'S WORK MAY SEEM IMPOSSIBLE. YET WE CAN DO ALL THINGS IN HIS STRENGTH.

BUT I STRONGLY BELIEVE WE CAN GO FURTHER. ALTHOUGH GOD'S WORK IS NOT EASY, IF WE TRUST HIM WHOLEHEARTEDLY, SUCCESS WILL DEFINITELY FOLLOW. HOWEVER, IF WE ONLY THINK OF GIVING IT A TRY, WE DON'T REALLY HAVE ENOUGH FAITH. GOD NEVER TELLS US TO TRY TO WORK, OR TRY TO GO. MERELY TRYING IS THE FIRST STEP TO FAILING.

OUR SINS AND WEAKNESS COME FROM OUR LACK OF FAITH. IF WE TRULY LOOK UP UPON THE LORD, HOW CAN WE NOT TRUST HIM? LET US BRAVELY AND FIRMLY FOLLOW GOD'S COMMANDS.

ABRAHAM TRUSTED GOD AND OFFERED HIS SON ISAAC. HE HAD FAITH THAT GOD WOULD BRING HIS SON BACK TO LIFE AGAIN.

MOSES TRUSTED GOD AND LED THE ISRAELITES ACROSS THE RED SEA.

JOSHUA TRUSTED GOD AND LED THE ISRAELITES ACROSS THE RIVER JORDAN TO GET TO CANAAN.

IT IS SATAN'S WORK TO MAKE PEOPLE DOUBT GOD'S WORDS, AND BLOCK OUR HEARTS FROM TRUSTING IN GOD. WHEN PEOPLE LOOK AT THEIR OWN WEAKNESS, THEY FAIL. YET GOD'S MIGHT BECOMES CLEAR IN TIMES OF WEAKNESS. IF WE TRULY BELIEVE THAT GOD IS WITH US, WE CAN DO GREAT THINGS FOR GOD.

HUDSON WAS GLAD TO HAVE THE SUPPORT OF HIS SISTER AND HER HUSBAND, WHO WERE WILLING TO TAKE CHARGE OF THE WORK IN MAINLAND CHINA. AT THE SAME TIME, HE RECRUITED ANOTHER 8 MISSIONARIES FOR CHINA.

RELATIONS BETWEEN CHINA AND BRITAIN WERE STRAINED, SO HUDSON'S FRIENDS SUGGESTED THAT HE WAIT IN ENGLAND UNTIL CHINA WAS SAFER.

HOWEVER, HUDSON DIDN'T LISTEN TO ADVICE, AND DECIDED TO SET OUT IN SEPTEMBER 1876.

IN YANTAI, THE BRITISH AMBASSADOR AND LI HONG ZHANG SIGNED A TREATY. IT ALLOWED FOREIGNERS TO TRAVEL AROUND AND LIVE IN CHINA.

THE TREATY PRESENTED THE MISSIONARIES WITH A GREAT OPPORTUNITY. FOR THE FIRST TIME THEY COULD TRAVEL FREELY THROUGHOUT CHINA. THEY TRAVELLED ENTHUSIASTICALLY FAR INLAND INTO DIFFERENT PROVINCES, PREACHING THE GOSPEL EVERYWHERE. THEY STILL HAD MANY DIFFICULTIES, BUT THEY ALSO HAD GREAT SUCCESS.

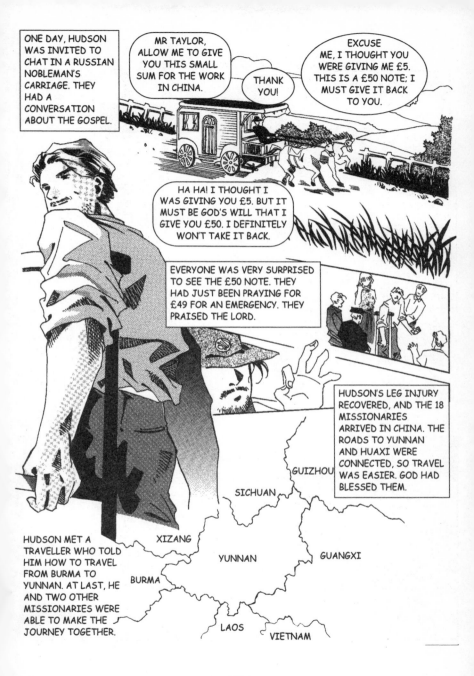

ONE DAY, HUDSON WAS INVITED TO CHAT IN A RUSSIAN NOBLEMAN'S CARRIAGE. THEY HAD A CONVERSATION ABOUT THE GOSPEL.

MR TAYLOR, ALLOW ME TO GIVE YOU THIS SMALL SUM FOR THE WORK IN CHINA.

THANK YOU!

EXCUSE ME, I THOUGHT YOU WERE GIVING ME £5. THIS IS A £50 NOTE; I MUST GIVE IT BACK TO YOU.

HA HA! I THOUGHT I WAS GIVING YOU £5. BUT IT MUST BE GOD'S WILL THAT I GIVE YOU £50. I DEFINITELY WON'T TAKE IT BACK.

EVERYONE WAS VERY SURPRISED TO SEE THE £50 NOTE. THEY HAD JUST BEEN PRAYING FOR £49 FOR AN EMERGENCY. THEY PRAISED THE LORD.

HUDSON'S LEG INJURY RECOVERED, AND THE 18 MISSIONARIES ARRIVED IN CHINA. THE ROADS TO YUNNAN AND HUAXI WERE CONNECTED, SO TRAVEL WAS EASIER. GOD HAD BLESSED THEM.

HUDSON MET A TRAVELLER WHO TOLD HIM HOW TO TRAVEL FROM BURMA TO YUNNAN. AT LAST, HE AND TWO OTHER MISSIONARIES WERE ABLE TO MAKE THE JOURNEY TOGETHER.

GUIZHOU
SICHUAN
XIZANG
YUNNAN
GUANGXI
BURMA
LAOS
VIETNAM

BUT SATAN WOULDN'T LET THEM GO EASILY, AND HE CAUSED DISAGREEMENTS AMONG THE MISSIONARIES. SO HUDSON ORGANISED A RETREAT CAMP, SO THE CHRISTIAN BROTHERS AND SISTERS COULD ESTABLISH BETTER RELATIONSHIPS. THEY FASTED AND PRAYED FOR GOD'S VICTORY OVER SATAN. THE CHURCHES WERE REVIVED, AND THEY WENT BACK TO THEIR WORK WITH JOY.

AT CHRISTMAS 1877, HUDSON RETURNED TO BRITAIN TO VISIT HIS FAMILY - SEVEN CHILDREN, ONE OF WHOM WAS AN ADOPTED DAUGHTER.

IRELAND

BRITAIN

LONDON

ALTHOUGH HE ENJOYED FAMILY LIFE, HUDSON NEVER FORGOT THE SPIRITUAL NEEDS OF CHINA. HE STARTED PLANNING TO SEND OUT ANOTHER 24 MALE MISSIONARIES AND 6 FEMALE MISSIONARIES.

PEOPLE AROUND THE WORLD HAD LEARNED OF THE WORK OF THE CHINA INLAND MISSION, AND OFFERINGS FLOODED IN. HOW SHOULD THE MONEY BE USED? AND WHO COULD TAKE IT TO CHINA? MRS TAYLOR WAS THE MOST SUITABLE CHOICE, BUT SHE WAS NEEDED TO CARE FOR THE CHILDREN AT HOME. AND WHO WOULD PAY HER TRAVELLING EXPENSES?

[HU]DSON [W]AS [P]RAYING FOR [TH]E 30 [MI]SSIONARIES [W]HEN HE [R]ECEIVED NEWS [AB]OUT A SEVERE [F]AMINE IN [N]ORTHERN CHINA.

THE NEXT DAY, THEY RECEIVED £10 TOWARDS TRAVELLING EXPENSES, AND ANOTHER £50 FOR FAMILY EXPENSES. THEY WERE ALSO GIVEN £1,000 TO ESTABLISH AN ORPHANAGE IN CHINA. HUDSON'S YOUNGER SISTER WAS LED BY THE SPIRIT TO OFFER TO CARE FOR THE HUDSON CHILDREN WITH HER OWN.

FINALLY, TWO FRIENDS PERSUADED HUDSON TO REST AND RECUPERATE IN SWITZERLAND, SO THAT MRS TAYLOR COULD GO TO CHINA WITHOUT WORRYING ABOUT HUDSON'S HEALTH. GOD HAD ORGANISED EVERYTHING! MRS TAYLOR AND HER TWO FEMALE COLLEAGUES SET OFF.

"MY DEAR WIFE, THE AIR IN SWITZERLAND IS VERY FRESH, AND I AM GRADUALLY RECOVERING. THANKS TO YOUR PRAYERS, GOD HAS GRANTED ME THIS TIME OF REST. GO ON WITH YOUR WORK FOR THE LORD'S SAKE. YOU ARE BLESSED EVERY DAY BY HIM."

BY THE END OF 1877, 28 OF THE 30 MISSIONARIES HAD LEFT FOR CHINA.

TWO PEOPLE TOOK OVER HUDSON'S WORK IN LONDON, ONE AS THE CHAIRMAN AND THE OTHER AS GENERAL EXECUTIVE COMMITTEE MEMBER. HUDSON WAS FREE TO LEAVE.

IN THE SPRING OF 1879, HUDSON RETURNED TO CHINA.

B. BROOMHALL

T. HOWARD

ON THE JOURNEY, HUDSON BECAME SERIOUSLY ILL ONCE MORE. A DOCTOR IN SINGAPORE SAID HE MIGHT NOT HAVE LONG TO LIVE.

SHANXI

SHANGHAI

～～ THE GREAT WALL.

MRS TAYLOR WAS AT THE ORPHANAGE WHEN SHE HEARD OF HUDSON'S ILLNESS. SHE LEFT HER WORK AND TRAVELLED TO SHANGHAI TO MEET HIM. FORTUNATELY, THE ORPHANAGE WAS WELL ESTABLISHED AND SHE FELT ABLE TO LEAVE SHANXI WITHOUT WORRY.

HUDSON GRADUALLY RECOVERED FROM HIS ILLNESS, AND HE WENT TO YAN TAI WITH HIS WIFE TO RECUPERATE. THEY INVITED TONG TO JOIN THEM. WHEN THEY SAW TONG'S CHILDREN PLAYING HAPPILY, THEY KNEW IT HAD BEEN A WISE DECISION.

DURING HIS CONVALESCENCE, HUDSON THOUGHT ABOUT BUYING LAND. IT WOULD BE A GOOD THING IF THEY COULD BUILD REST HOMES AND SCHOOLS.

GOD ARRANGED FOR THEM TO BUY SOME LAND CHEAPLY, AND THEY DECIDED TO DESIGN AND SUPERVISE THE CONSTRUCTION WORK THEMSELVES. AT LAST, THE FAMOUS YAN TAI SCHOOL WAS ESTABLISHED.

WHEN HUDSON FIRST ARRIVED IN CHINA, PEOPLE OBJECTED TO FEMALE MISSIONARIES. NOW THE SITUATION WAS TOTALLY DIFFERENT. THERE WERE 30 FEMALE MISSIONARIES IN GUANGXIN AREA, AND THEY ALL ENJOYED RESPECT AND SUPPORT.

MRS LEE LIVED IN CHONGQING. SHE REPORTED THAT SEVERAL HUNDRED VISITORS ARRIVED EVERY DAY, LISTENING EAGERLY TO THE PREACHING.

ZHANGSHA

HUNAN

MISS KATE SAID, "I LIKE THESE HUNANESE LADIES. THEY ARE SO KIND, AND THEY WELCOME US INTO THEIR HOMES."

ONCE WHEN I WAS PREACHING ALONE OUTSIDE, THEY LED ME TO THEIR HOMES AND TOOK CARE OF ME. THEY'RE KIND AND THOUGHTFUL. MAY GOD BLESS THEM.

DON'T BE AFRAID, WE'LL LOOK AFTER YOU.

TWO MISSIONARIES ON THEIR WAY TO SHANXI SAID, "WE ARE ALWAYS WELL TREATED BY THE PEOPLE THERE. THEY TRY THEIR BEST TO MAKE US FEEL COMFORTABLE AND SERVE US WARMLY. THANK GOD."

THE LADIES' WORK HAS ACHIEVED A LOT, BUT THERE HAVE BEEN MANY SACRIFICES. IN 1881, MRS KIM DIED, LEAVING BEHIND HER NEWBORN BABY. IN GUIZHOU, MRS HUA AND HER CHILD BOTH DIED. AT THE POINT OF DEATH, SHE SAID, "IT S A PITY THAT I COULDN'T DO VERY MUCH. I KNOW THAT AFTER I DIE, OTHERS, MORE CAPABLE THAN I, WILL COME TO SERVE CHINA."

HUDSON ENCOURAGED THE FEMALE MISSIONARIES. "YOUR WORK AMONG THE WOMEN IS SO IMPORTANT. ONLY YOU CAN VISIT THEM IN THEIR HOMES AND TELL THEM ABOUT GOD."

THE CHINESE LADIES SAID, "YOU WARM OUR HEARTS. WE HAVE NEVER FELT SUCH LOVE, NOT EVEN IN OUR PARENTS' HOME."

IN 1881, THE MISSION PUBLISHED NEW GUIDELINES. "DEVOTE YOURSELVES TO GOD AND STAY CLOSE TO HIM, SEEKING HIS WILL AND FOLLOWING HIS COMMANDS. ONLY GOD CAN HELP US TO BEAR THE BURDEN OF THIS RESPONSIBILITY. THE GOD WE SERVE WILL NEVER FAIL US."

A SPECIAL WELCOME MEETING WAS HELD FOR THE 70 NEW WORKERS WHO CAME TO CHINA.

IN AUTUMN 1881, HUDSON'S FATHER AND HIS WIFE'S MOTHER DIED. HUDSON'S WIFE WENT BACK TO THE UK IN OCTOBER.

IN DECEMBER, THE CHINESE PRAYED FOR THE NEW MISSIONARIES WHO WERE NOW IN ZHENG JIANG

"I THANKED GOD THAT MY PARENTS WERE CALLED TO BE WITH HIM IN HEAVEN, AND THEY WOULD NOT FEEL PAIN OR SADNESS ANY MORE."

IN 1882 A SERIOUS FINANCIAL PROBLEM AROSE.

WE WERE EXPECTING ABOUT £7,000 - BUT ONLY £96 HAS BEEN RECEIVED! LORD! WHAT CAN WE DO? PLEASE HELP US RESOLVE THIS PROBLEM.

- GOD IS LOVE. -

THE LOVE OF OUR FATHER IS SO GREAT. WE KEPT ASKING AND BEGGING HIM TO SEND US A WEALTHY DONOR TO MEET OUR NEEDS. WE ASKED GOD TO BLESS HIM AND HIS FAMILY. WE KNEW GOD WOULD MOVE IN HIS POWER, AND WE TRUSTED HIM TO HELP US.

OUR COLLEAGUES IN YAN TAI PRAYED TOGETHER. AS THEY EXPECTED, GOD HELPED THEM. LOCAL PEOPLE GAVE DONATIONS WHICH COVERED THEIR EXPENSES FOR NOVEMBER AND DECEMBER.

FATHER: £1,000
MOTHER: £1,000
AMELIA: £200
ROSY: £200
BROTHER: £200
SISTER: £200
HENRY: £200

IN FEBRUARY 1883, HUDSON SAILED FOR ENGLAND. HE CARRIED WITH HIM A LETTER FROM HIS SISTER-IN-LAW, TELLING HIM OF THE GENEROSITY OF HIS FAMILY AND FRIENDS. THREE THOUSAND POUNDS FOR THE MISSION!

GOD WOULD REMEMBER THEIR GENEROSITY.

MR AND MRS TAYLOR MET UP IN FRANCE, AND TRAVELLED BACK TO ENGLAND.

HUDSON WAS WELCOMED IN ENGLAND AND WAS INVITED TO PREACH IN MANY PLACES.

AT THE END OF 1883 HE HAD 70 NEW WORKERS SAILING FOR CHINA.

ENCOURAGED BY THE ACTIVITY OF THESE OUTSTANDING WORKERS, MORE AND MORE YOUNG PEOPLE CAME TO CHINA TO PREACH. DURING 1883 AND 1884 EVERYTHING RAN SMOOTHLY AND THE CHINA INLAND MISSION RECEIVED LOTS OF DONATIONS. NUMBERS IN THE CHURCHES GREW. GOD'S WORK WAS GREATER THAN PEOPLE EVER HOPED OR IMAGINED.

IN MARCH 1885 SEVEN STUDENTS SAILED FOR CHINA.

C. T. STUDD
STANLEY SMITH
MONTAGU BEAUCHAMP
D. E. HOSTE
W. W. CASSELS
CECIL POLHILL-TURNER
ARTHUR POHILL-TURNER

THEY BECAME KNOWN AS THE CAMBRIDGE SEVEN, AND THEY ALL DID OUTSTANDING WORK IN CHINA.

A CHINA COUNCIL WAS FOUNDED IN 1885 IN NORTH CHINA TO HELP NEW ARRIVALS SETTLE IN TO THEIR NEW LIFE-WORK.

HERBERT

PASTOR HSI

THE MISSIONARIES COMMUNICATED WELL WITH THE CHINESE, HELPING AND CARING FOR THEM, AND MAKING PERSONAL SACRIFICES TO DO SO. MANY PEOPLE BEGAN TO BELIEVE IN GOD AT THE HOSPITAL TRAINING SCHOOLS. THEY LEARNED TO TRUST IN GOD, AND RELY TOTALLY ON HIM. THEY LEARNED THAT THE GOSPEL IS THE MOST IMPORTANT THING IN LIFE, AND THEY LEARNED TO PRAISE AND GLORIFY GOD IN EVERYTHING.

FOUR OF THE CAMBRIDGE SEVEN WENT TO PINGYANG WHERE THEY MET EX-CONFUCIAN SCHOLAR PASTOR HSI.

THANK GOD FOR GIVING US FOOD.

"SOMEONE IS SELLING FOOD."

MEANWHILE HUDSON AND MONTAGU BEAUCHAMP WERE ON THE WAY TO HANZHONG.

"WHERE IS IT?"

NO MATTER WHERE MR HUDSON WAS, HE ALWAYS GOT UP TO PRAY AT DAYBREAK AND WAS NEVER INTERRUPTED.

AFTER A SHORT TIME STAYING IN HANZHONG, HUDSON WENT BACK TO SHANGHAI TO ATTEND AN EMERGENCY MEETING THERE. HE ARRANGED FOR EVERY DIRECTOR FROM EVERY PROVINCE TO ATTEND AN ADVANCED TEACHING PROGRAMME.

SHANGHAI COMMITTEE

WE PRAYED WITH ALL OUR HEART FOR GOD TO SEND ONE HUNDRED MISSIONARIES TO CHINA IN 1887, AND WE ALSO HOPED TO GET AT LEAST £1,000 IN DONATIONS.

ALL THE COMMISSIONERS THOUGHT IT WAS IMPOSSIBLE, BUT HUDSON GREW IN CONFIDENCE AND KEPT ON PRAYING FOR THE COMING OF "THE ONE HUNDRED".

"I AM PLEASED TO HEAR THAT YOU PRAY FOR THE COMING OF THESE NEW WORKERS, BUT IT IS NOT EASY TO GET SO MANY IN JUST ONE YEAR. WHATEVER NUMBERS WE RECEIVE WE SHOULD FEEL HAPPY."

"WE ARE SO JOYFUL IN HAVING ONE HUNDRED MISSIONARIES. I PROMISED THAT YOU WOULD SEE THEM IF GOD KEPT YOU ALIVE."

A CHURCHMAN IN SHANGHAI.

"SINCE 1887, MANY DONATIONS HAVE BEEN RECEIVED, MAKING £11,000 IN TOTAL. SIX HUNDRED PEOPLE OFFERED TO SERVE IN CHINA, BUT ONLY 102 COULD ACTUALLY GO. SEVERAL OF THE OLD MISSIONARIES DIED SHORTLY AFTER THEY WELCOMED THESE NEW WORKERS."

IN 1888, HUDSON VISITED NEW YORK, WHERE HE MET HIS BROTHER WHO RESPECTED HIM VERY MUCH.

H.W. FROST

AFTERWARDS HUDSON WENT BACK TO LONDON. LATER HE AND HIS WIFE JENNIE WERE INVITED BACK TO AMERICA

HUDSON PREACHED IN SUMMER MEETINGS IN NEW YORK, TORONTO AND CHICAGO. ALL THESE MEETINGS WERE WELL ATTENDED.

"HEARING HUDSON TAYLOR PREACH WAS LIKE RECEIVING A REVELATION FROM GOD."

"LOOK, MR HUDSON, THESE EVANGELICALS ARE SO ENTHUSIASTIC! THEY HAVE DONATED ENOUGH TO SUPPORT EIGHT MISSIONARIES IN CHINA."

MR HUDSON WAS NOT SO HAPPY. HE FELT UNDER PRESSURE.

THANKS BE TO GOD!

"MY DEAR AMERICAN FRIENDS, I WOULD NOT WORRY IF ONE MISSIONARY COULD NOT GET ENOUGH MONEY, BECAUSE GOD WOULD PREPARE OTHERS WILLING TO HELP FINANCIALLY. BUT IT WOULD BE SERIOUS IF PEOPLE ONLY WANTED TO DONATE MONEY AND NOT TO SERVE THEMSELVES. LOVE IS NOT MERELY ABOUT MONEY, IT IS ABOUT PEOPLE WILLING TO GIVE UP THEIR LIVES AND GO TO PREACH THE GOSPEL."

IN A SHORT PERIOD OF TIME OVER 40 PEOPLE HAD OFFERED TO SERVE IN CHINA. ONLY EIGHT OF THEM WERE FINALLY ACCEPTED, AND THEY WERE ABLE TO SUPPORT THEMSELVES. SO MONEY WAS IN SURPLUS. IT SEEMED AS IF THE MONEY GIVEN TO GOD WAS LIKE THE FISH AND BREAD JESUS USED TO FEED THE 5,000 – IT NEVER CAME TO AN END.

HUDSON'S SUCCESS WAS DUE TO HIS HUMILITY. HE WAS NEVER OVER-CONFIDENT, NO MATTER WHAT HE HAD TO DEAL WITH. HE ALWAYS PRAYED TO GOD TO HELP HIM SUCCEED.

WHEN HUDSON CAME BACK FROM NORTH AMERICA, HE GUESSED THAT HE WOULD FACE SOME BIG CHALLENGES. FIRST HE HEARD THAT SOME CIM MISSIONARIES HAD DIED, AND MORE BAD NEWS FOLLOWED THAT. HIS COLLEAGUES ON THE BRITISH COUNCIL WERE OPPOSED TO HIM SETTING UP A BRANCH IN AMERICA. FORTUNATELY, THEY CHANGED THEIR MINDS WHEN HE EXPLAINED HIS THINKING.

IN JULY 1889, AN ASSISTANT COUNCIL WAS FOUNDED IN GLASGOW, SCOTLAND, TO HELP MISSIONARIES GET TO CHINA MORE EASILY. A WOMEN'S BRANCH WAS FOUNDED IN LONDON TO PROVIDE THEM WITH TRAINING OPPORTUNITIES.

LONDON

HUDSON TAYLOR WAS IN AMERICA AT THAT TIME AND HE HAD ALREADY PREACHED OVER FORTY TIMES IN EIGHTEEN PLACES.

HE WAS EVEN INVITED TO VISIT SWEDEN BY THE SWEDISH QUEEN.

"WE CALL ON GOD TO PERSUADE CHRISTIANS FROM ALL OVER THE WORLD TO SEND A THOUSAND MISSIONARIES TO CHINA WITHIN FIVE YEARS. FOR THOUSANDS OF CHINESE NEED JESUS. WE NEED YOU TO SERVE THERE AND WE WILL SEE SUCCESS IF WE RELY ON JESUS ALONE. "GO AND MAKE DISCIPLES OF ALL NATIONS." (MATTHEW 28:19)

HUDSON TAYLOR ORIGINALLY THOUGHT SEVERAL MISSIONARIES WOULD BE ENOUGH TO SERVE IN CHINA, BUT HE FOUND HE WAS TOTALLY WRONG. CHINA IS A HUGE COUNTRY, AND A FEW MISSIONARIES WERE NOT ENOUGH. HUDSON WANTED EVERY CHINESE PERSON TO HEAR THE GOSPEL. NOW CHINA AND BRITAIN WERE MORE CONNECTED THAN EVER BEFORE, AND HE BELIEVED THAT THIS GREAT NATION COULD BE WON FOR GOD IF ALL THE EVANGELICALS WERE UNITED.

A CUTTING FROM A CHINESE NEWSPAPER SAID: THERE ARE ALMOST FIVE HUNDRED MISSIONARIES READY TO TEACH THE CHINESE PEOPLE.

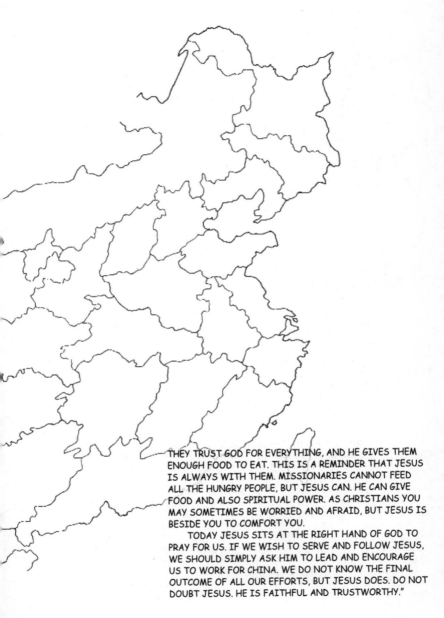

THEY TRUST GOD FOR EVERYTHING, AND HE GIVES THEM
ENOUGH FOOD TO EAT. THIS IS A REMINDER THAT JESUS
IS ALWAYS WITH THEM. MISSIONARIES CANNOT FEED
ALL THE HUNGRY PEOPLE, BUT JESUS CAN. HE CAN GIVE
FOOD AND ALSO SPIRITUAL POWER. AS CHRISTIANS YOU
MAY SOMETIMES BE WORRIED AND AFRAID, BUT JESUS IS
BESIDE YOU TO COMFORT YOU.

TODAY JESUS SITS AT THE RIGHT HAND OF GOD TO
PRAY FOR US. IF WE WISH TO SERVE AND FOLLOW JESUS,
WE SHOULD SIMPLY ASK HIM TO LEAD AND ENCOURAGE
US TO WORK FOR CHINA. WE DO NOT KNOW THE FINAL
OUTCOME OF ALL OUR EFFORTS, BUT JESUS DOES. DO NOT
DOUBT JESUS. HE IS FAITHFUL AND TRUSTWORTHY."

AT THAT TIME GOD'S WORD WAS SPREADING ALL OVER THE WORLD. COMMUNITIES IN AUSTRALIA, EUROPE AND AMERICA WERE ALL TAKING SERIOUSLY THEIR RESPONSIBILITY TO GET "CHINA BACK TO GOD". THEY CONTACTED THE CHINA INLAND MISSION TO HELP WITH THIS GREAT WORK.

DISCIPLES SET UP A BRANCH OF CIM IN AUSTRALIA. THEY ALSO ORGANISED A GERMAN-CHINESE ALLIANCE AND A SWISS-CHINESE ALLIANCE. WITHIN SIX MONTHS, 103 NEW MISSIONARIES WENT TO SHANGHAI.

AS SOON AS HUDSON TAYLOR CAME TO AUSTRALIA AROUND 60 PEOPLE OFFERED TO SERVE IN CHINA.

1890

WE ARE EAGER TO SUPPORT THE WORK OF CIM.

SATAN IMMEDIATELY WENT ON THE ATTACK. SOON THERE WAS RIOTING IN THE REGION ALONG THE YANGTZE RIVER. AS A RESULT, MANY CHURCHES WERE DESTROYED.

AS THE MISSIONARIES FACED SATAN'S ATTACKS, THE PEOPLE COULD SEE THAT THEY WERE WILLING TO SACRIFICE EVERYTHING FOR GOD, AND WERE PREPARED TO BE FAITHFUL UNTIL THE END. EVEN DURING HARD TIMES, THEIR WORDS AND ACTIONS WERE TRUE TO THE GOSPEL, AND THEY RELIED ON GOD'S POWER RATHER THAN MILITARY MIGHT. AS THEY SUFFERED FOR GOD THEY SET A GOOD EXAMPLE FOR THE CHINESE DISCIPLES.

DURING THIS DIFFICULT PERIOD, IT WAS HARDER TO FIND REGULAR TIMES FOR PRAYER. HUDSON HUMBLY ASKED HIMSELF WHETHER HE HAD DONE ANYTHING WRONG TO CAUSE AN OBSTACLE TO GOD'S BLESSING.

HE BEGAN TO WONDER ABOUT THE AUTHORITY IN THE CHINA INLAND MISSION. SHOULD BRITAIN BE IN CHARGE, OR CHINA? AFTER MUCH PRAYER, HE DECIDED THAT AUTHORITY SHOULD BE GIVEN TO THE CHINESE.

"EXPANDING OUR CHURCHES AND OUR MEMBERSHIP IS NO USE IF GOD DOES NOT APPROVE OUR WORK. I BEGGED GOD TO EXAMINE OUR THOUGHTS AND PURIFY OUR MINDS. I KNEW HE WOULD FORGIVE US IF WE ADMITTED OUR WEAKNESS AND SINS. THEN WE COULD DEVOTE OURSELVES ONCE AGAIN TO SERVING HIM."

Faithful Servant

Hudson aged 62–73

PROGRESS CONTINUED: HUDSON WENT TO GERMANY TWICE, AND ALSO RECRUITED YOUNG MEN FROM THE UK AND RUSSIA. THE PUBLICATION OF A BRIEF HISTORY OF THE CHINA INLAND MISSION WAS VERY INFLUENTIAL.

A BRIEF HISTORY OF THE CIM

LONDON

IN 1893, HUDSON WENT TO NORTHERN CHINA TO RESOLVE AN ARGUMENT. IT WAS A HOT, EXHAUSTING JOURNEY.

DAD, ARE YOU OK? IT'S BEEN A LONG, HARD JOURNEY, HASN'T IT?

DAUGHTER-IN-LAW. CHENEE.

YES, WE HAVE TO MAKE SACRIFICES FOR OUR FRIENDS.

"WITHOUT HUDSON WE WOULD NOT KNOW THE LOVE OF GOD."

WHEN THE MISSIONARIES PASSED THROUGH HENAN PROVINCE THEY WERE TREATED WITH GREAT HOSPITALITY.

I OFTEN REMIND MYSELF HOW PRECIOUS OUR OLD CLERGYMEN ARE. I AM NOT OLD AND MAY HAVE ONE OR TWO DECADES TO GO. GOD, IF I SHOULD DIE SUDDENLY, PLEASE GIVE MY LEFT-OVER YEARS TO THEM. I WOULD BE HAPPY TO GIVE MY TIME FOR THEIRS.

142

I WENT TO PINYANG AND CESHANMO WELCOMED ME.

WHEN I SEE ALL THE PROBLEMS YOU HAVE FACED, AND ALL THAT YOU HAVE ACHIEVED, I FEEL HUMBLE. IT IS MY HONOUR TO SERVE YOU.

THE CHINA-JAPAN WAR STARTED IN 1894, BUT HUDSON WAS STILL PRAYING FOR HIS 1000 MISSIONARIES. IN THE END A TOTAL OF 1,153 MISSIONARIES WERE SENT TO CHINA OVER A FIVE-YEAR PERIOD. HUDSON REMINDED THE CHURCHES THAT THE WORK WAS NOT COMPLETED – THERE WAS STILL SO MUCH TO DO.

THERE WAS BAD NEWS FROM THE INNER AREAS: THE MUSLIMS IN SICHUAN AND QINGHAI PROVINCES HAD STARTED A REVOLUTION. MANY PEOPLE HAD BEEN INJURED OR KILLED, AND THE CHINA INLAND MISSION WAS TRYING ITS BEST TO HELP THE VICTIMS. THE CHINESE DISCIPLES TRIED BRAVELY TO SAVE THE FOREIGN MISSIONARIES.

BRITISH CHRISTIANS WERE STILL PRAYING FOR CHINA, AND DURING THESE HARD TIMES EVEN MORE PEOPLE WERE BEING SAVED. THROUGHOUT THE WORLD, GOD SEEMED TO BE ENCOURAGING PEOPLE TO FOCUS ON CHINA.

GOD WAS HELPING US EVERYWHERE, AND BRINGING US COMFORT.

HUDSON WAS NOW 64 YEARS OLD. HE KNEW HE WAS GETTING WEAKER, SO HE CONCENTRATED ON FINDING THE LEADERS WHO COULD TAKE OVER FROM HIM. HE SET UP DIRECTORS IN EVERY PROVINCE AND APPOINTED TALENTED PEOPLE TO TAKE CHARGE IN EACH AREA.

HE MADE A VISIT TO INDIA AND THEN RETURNED TO SHANGHAI, WHERE HE ASKED PASTOR GU TO REPRESENT HIM AS A DIRECTOR. HE RETURNED TO THE UK ON A PREACHING TOUR, AND THEN WENT ON TO FRANCE. HIS HEALTH WAS POOR AND HE NEEDED A REST.

EVEN THEN, HE ACCEPTED INVITATIONS TO TALK ABOUT THE MISSION. HE WENT TO GERMANY, WHERE THE CLERGY DISTRUSTED THE POLICIES OF THE CHINA INLAND MISSION. THEY WERE INITIALLY UNFRIENDLY TOWARDS HUDSON.

145

WE FEEL ASHAMED IN FRONT OF HIM.

AFTER THE TRIP TO GERMANY, HUDSON WAS KEPT BUSY IN THE UK: THE CHINA INLAND MISSION HAD GREAT FINANCIAL PROBLEMS. HUDSON PRAYED URGENTLY TO GOD, AND RECEIVED £2,000 FROM A MISSIONARY NAMED MU. HE WAS SURPRISED TO RECEIVE A FURTHER £100,000 WHEN MU DIED. REMEMBERING THAT SOULS CANNOT BE SAVED WITHOUT MISSIONARIES, HUDSON WENT ON PRAYING FOR MISSIONARIES FILLED WITH GOD'S LOVE AND POWER.

"IT IS 1898, AND I HAVE MADE TEN VISITS TO CHINA. ALL THIS TIME I HAVE PRAYED FOR GOD TO HELP THE CHINESE CHRISTIANS LEAD GOOD LIVES AND BE USED BY HIM. THAT TIME WHEN 1,000 MISSIONARIES CAME TO CHINA AND SATAN GOT HIS REVENGE TAUGHT US A LESSON: DO NOT GO BACK NO MATTER WHAT HAPPENS. TRUST IN GOD."

"I HAVE OFTEN BEEN ILL, BUT IT'S GOOD TO SEE THAT GOD'S BUSINESS IS STILL GOING FORWARD WITHOUT ME. GOD HAS GIVEN ME MORE TIME TO TALK AND PRAY WITH MY COLLEAGUES, SO WE CAN SOW MORE SEEDS FOR THE FUTURE."

HUDSON LAID PLANS, WROTE LETTERS AND INTERVIEWED CANDIDATES FOR THE MISSION.

1900

MILITARY GROUPS INVADED BEIJING AND TIANJING THEN DESTROYED YUANMINGYUAN. THERE WAS UNREST EVERYWHERE.

EMPRESS DOWAGER CIXI PUT EMPEROR GUANGXU UNDER HOUSE ARREST. AN IMPERIAL DECREE ORDERED THE DEATH OF ALL FOREIGNERS, RESULTING IN THE MURDER OF HUNDREDS OF CHRISTIANS. THE CHINA INLAND MISSION ALONE SAW 58 ADULTS AND 21 CHILDREN MARTYRED FOR THEIR FAITH.

THIS BAD NEWS SADDENED HUDSON DEEPLY AND MADE HIM VERY ILL. EVEN THOUGH SO MANY OF THEIR PEOPLE HAD DIED, THE CHINA INLAND MISSION DID NOT COMPLAIN. THE UK MINISTRY OF FOREIGN AFFAIRS AND THE EMBASSY IN BEIJING ADMIRED THEM FOR IT.

IN 1902, HE RESIGNED HIS DIRECTORSHIP OF THE MISSION. HE WAS SUCCEEDED BY D.E. HOSTE, ONE OF THE CAMBRIDGE SEVEN.

HUDSON REMAINED IN SWITZERLAND, RESTING AND STUDYING HIS BIBLE, BUT CHINA WAS ALWAYS CLOSE TO HIS HEART AND IN HIS PRAYERS.

IN 1903 MRS TAYLOR BECAME ILL. HER DOCTORS DECIDED THAT AN OPERATION WAS UNSAFE, AND SHE REMAINED SERIOUSLY SICK.

EVEN WHEN SHE WAS DYING, SHE CONTINUED TO WRITE TO RELATIVES AND FRIENDS TO ENCOURAGE THEM. HER LAST ACT WAS TO DONATE A HUNDRED POUNDS TO THE CHINA INLAND MISSION.

SHE WAS AT PEACE.

"THERE IS NO PAIN."

PLEASE, GOD, SET HER FREE QUICKLY.

HUDSON NEVER PRAYED SUCH A DIFFICULT PRAYER. FIVE MINUTES LATER, HIS WIFE STOPPED BREATHING. SAD AND LONELY, HE WEPT BITTERLY.

BUT HE KNEW THAT GOD WAS HIS STRENGTH, AND HE DRIED HIS TEARS.

那應許我們的是信實的．

IN 1905

HUDSON, HIS SECOND SON HOWARD AND HIS DAUGHTER-IN-LAW GERALDINE WENT TO SHANGHAI AGAIN IN APRIL.

THEY MET UP WITH SOME CHURCH FRIENDS, AND A FEW DAYS LATER THEY VISITED THE MISSIONARY CEMETERY. THEY KNEW THAT ONE DAY THEY WOULD MEET ALL THEIR FRIENDS AGAIN.

HUDSON ARRIVED IN CHEN JOU TO A TREMENDOUS WELCOME FROM THE BELIEVERS THERE. THEY GAVE HIM A LENGTH OF SILK ON WHICH THEY HAD INSCRIBED THEIR LOVE AND THANKS.

A GREAT LEADER.

WELCOME HUDSON TAYLOR!

EPHESIANS 3:10-13

"GOD REGARDS THE CHURCH
AS THE CENTRE OF HIS PLAN,
ACHIEVING HIS PURPOSES
THROUGH IT. EVERY
MISSIONARY HAS HIS OR
HER PART TO PLAY, WORKING
ACCORDING TO HIS NAME.
THE HEAD OF THE CHURCH IS
CHRIST, AND CHRIST IS
EVERYTHING TO US."

HUDSON TAYLOR'S PIONEERING WORK IN CHINA SOWED THE SEED OF THE GOSPEL THROUGHOUT THE LAND. HE ENCOURAGED THE CHINESE CHRISTIANS TO TAKE ON THE LEADERSHIP OF THE CHURCH, AND TO FOLLOW THE EXAMPLE OF THE FOREIGN MISSIONARIES, GIVING UP THEIR OWN INTERESTS FOR THE SAKE OF OTHERS, LIKE THEIR LORD AND MASTER JESUS CHRIST.

"WE HAVE LIVED IN THE WORLD, AND RECEIVED LOVING KINDNESS FROM GOD AND SHARE FOREVER IN THE HAPPINESS ALLOTTED TO US BY OUR DESTINY. WE HAVE TO KNOW THE PURPOSE OF OUR LIFE AND REALISE THE LOVE OF LEADING PEOPLE AND ENJOY SHARING THE GOSPEL WITH PEOPLE, SEEING, HOW FORTUNATE WE ARE. WE'VE GOT GOD TO BE OUR MASSIVE ROCK AND SHELTER AND HELP. WE DON'T WANT TO STAY AN INFANT FOREVER BUT TO BE CHRISTIAN SOLDIERS AND LIVE A LIFE OF NO REGRETS."

HUDSON TAYLOR CELEBRATED HIS 73RD BIRTHDAY ON 21ST MAY, 1905.

HENAN

KEIFENG

JIANGSU

HE BEI

NANJING

HANKOU

WU HAN

BIBLE

IN APRIL 1905 HUDSON VISITED THE CEMETERY AT YANG HSIA.

26TH MAY 1905 WAS THE 39TH ANNIVERSARY OF THE SAILING OF THE LAMMERMUIR, THE SHIP THAT BROUGHT THE FIRST MISSIONARY TEAM TO CHINA.

ON 1ST JUNE 1905 HE TRAVELLED TO CHANG HSIA.

ON 2ND JUNE THERE WAS HEAVY RAIN ALL DAY.

ON THE AFTERNOON OF 3RD JUNE, HUDSON MET SOME CHURCH FRIENDS. AFTERWARDS HE WAS VERY TIRED, SO HIS DAUGHTER-IN-LAW TOOK HIS MEAL UP TO HIS ROOM.

SHE STOOD SILENTLY IN HIS ROOM, NOT SAYING A WORD.

HA.

155

CHINESE AND FOREIGN FRIENDS CAME TO SAY THEIR LAST FAREWELLS. THEY KNEW THAT ONE DAY THEY WOULD SEE HIM AGAIN.

HE WAS BURIED, IN ACCORDANCE WITH HIS WISHES, WITH HIS WIFE BESIDE THE YANGTZE RIVER.

HUDSON HAD GONE HOME TO GLORY, AND WAS IN HIS FATHER'S HOUSE AT LAST.

THE END OF THE STORY OF A GREAT MAN.